Story:

The Language of Faith

Mason Olds

Copyright © 1977 by

University Press of America™

division of
R.F. Publishing, Inc.
4710 Auth Place, S.E., Washington, D.C. 20023

0-8191-0228-8

GOD'S IN HIS HEAVEN

He sits up there cross-legged
Arms resting on his belly,
Laughing.

Long white beard upon white nightshirt
Bouncing up and down--
He laughs.

From throne of tattered cloud
The laughter's scarcely heard,
Then fades.

Marjorie Olds

To

Marjorie

who knows the sound of silence

Preface

Publications and courses in theology and literature have been around for some time. What they attempt to do is to overcome the isolation and specialization of the two distinct disciplines and to relate them to one another. Scholars such as Nathan A. Scott, Jr., Amos Wilder, Stanley Hopper, Randall Stewart and others have shown that such an attempt can be rigorous, insightful, interesting, and with benefits which accrue to both disciplines.

Since the proclamation by some radical theologians in the early 1960s that "God is dead", the interest in theology and literature has greatly accelerated. It--along with process theology, liberation theology, and theology of play--seems to be a genuine response to the allegation about the passing away of the late God. Evidences of this new interest are amply seen in the works of such scholars as Sallie TeSalle, Giles Gunn, John Dunne, James Wiggins and many others.

My study, then, is in the general area of religious thought and modern literature. What these two terms mean specifically will be spelled out later in this study. This work reveals another voice in the growing chorus of voices which speak from a broad common perspective.

As a preview to what follows, the first two chapters deal with perspective. In a sense the first chapter is a brief prolegomenon to theology and literature, making the claim that story is a legitimate means for conveying religious faith, and the second chapter outlines the salient features of the Christian story. The next four chapters give an analysis of the human condition under the categories of sin, suffering, and death. Under the category of "Christ paradigm", chapter five attempts to provide a Christian answer for coping with the human condition. The work closes with a final chapter which serves as a kind of epilogue or even a postlude in that it takes some of the insights gleaned from Good Friday and Easter and uses them to illuminate modern woman's experience of the silence of God.

Of course, a work such as this has been influenced either directly or indirectly by the scholarly efforts of others. Where the dependency is obvious, I have tried to acknowledge it. However, there are some who have contributed to this work in other ways and deserve special acknowledgment here. I am indebted to Springfield College for granting me a sabbatical leave (1975) so that I might have the time for study and writing, and I also am indebted to its Research Fund Committee for providing me with a grant which provided for the original typing of the manuscript. Furthermore, I owe a special debt to professors Edward Sims of the English Department and Holmes Vanderbeck and Robert Kitchen of the Religion and Philosophy Department at Springfield College for

carefully reading the work and offering their helpful suggestions for

improvement. And above all, I owe very much to my wife, Marjorie,

who has read and re-read the manuscript and offered valuable suggestions

as to style. It is to her that this work is dedicated.

Mason Olds
Amherst, Massachusetts

CONTENTS

CHAPTER I

POINT OF VIEW

There have been many attempts to define the essence of
man. He is an animal who thinks, or who plays, or who laughs,
or who dances, or who creates, or who knows he will die.
To a certain extent, all of these characteristics contain
an element of truth, but I wish to suggest another aspect
of man's nature, namely, he is an animal who tells stories.

Man tells many stories, and often within the story told
there are a number of secondary stories. There is, for instance, the story of my life; but within my story there are
numerous minor stories. Some of these lesser stories are:
the story of my maleness, or my white middle classness, of
my vocation as a college professor, and of my religious faith.
Just as I have my story, others have their stories, some of
these are: the story of women's liberation, the blacks'
story of the struggle for racial equality, and the story of
the poor man's attempt to survive. These stories impinge
upon my story, and often have the consequences of lifting my
level of consciousness; so that when I tell my story in the
future it is somewhat altered.[1]

---

[1] Robert McAfee Brown, "Story and Theology," Philosophy
of Religion and Theology: 1974, compiled by James W. Mc-
Clendon, Jr. (Missoula: Scholars Press, 1974), pp. 55-72.
Brown has worked out very carefully the relationship of story
to theological reflection, and I am generally in agreement
with his statement.

The story of my faith is connected with the Christian story, which has impinged upon me just as other stories have. Likewise the Christian story has lifted my level of consciousness and has become a part of my story. But the mediation between the Christian story and my story is not a one way street. As the Christian story has become a part of my story, my story in some small way has become a part of the Christian story. Just as I cannot extricate myself from the Christian story completely, even if I want to, neither can it separate itself from me. Should I revile against the Christian story and opt for atheism, my atheism would be Christian atheism. For better or worse, my story and the Christian story are a part of each other, although I may publicly and formally repudiate it and even if its earthly representatives should formally cast me from its membership. This is true because it has played a part in molding my consciousness and thus has influenced my story. In a similar way, my presence at worship services, my singing the hymns, my theological discussions with other Christians, even my financial contributions--all of these as infinitesimal and as discordant as they may be--cannot be miraculously and abruptly eradicated.

This study then is an essay in constructive religious thought via contemporary drama and the novel. It is an attempt to reflect seriously on the Christian story and its individual sub-stories which come together to develop its plot. Yet it is not my desire to simply retell the stories of the past, but rather it is an attempt to express the fundamental meaning of the story in terms of contemporary stories. In other words, I, as the reflector, shall seek to bridge the gap between the message of the story, told in the past, and the contemporary listener of stories. The old story, in a sense, will be retold with contemporary stories, the aim being to overcome the alienation that exists between the past and the present. As my concern is for both theology and literature, I shall first explain their relationship to one another.

1. Theology and Literature

Theology is reflection on the Christian story, or it is faith reflecting on itself. The theologian is a man of faith who steps back and thinks about the faith. Faith is a primary activity, whereas theology is a secondary one. Without theology faith becomes static, irrelevant and dies. But without faith, the theologian has no personal commitment to the faith he is thinking about and wishes to explain. He is simply doing history of religion. Hence the theologian is a person who is committed to the faith he is reflecting upon.

The task of theology has to be done in every age. The theological thinking of the Medieval period is not adequate for the problems that confront us today. History moves on, and new philosophies and ideologies arise. New sciences come into existence, and with them new ways to perceive the

world assert themselves. Even new states of consciousness
come into being. Things that were taken for granted are now
questioned. The old morality is forced to step aside as the
new morality seeks to have its fling. As the old expression
of faith encounters the novel, it has to be rethought.
Otherwise it becomes intellectually obsolete and irrelevant,
not so much because it is not true, but because of the out-
dated style in which it is expressed.

As the theologian reflects on the Christian story, a
number of subjects demand his attention. First, he thinks
on the being and nature of God, and once he entertains this
fundamental subject he opens a theological Pandora's box,
which releases other important subjects that force themselves
upon him. Immediately the problem of revelation asserts
itself with its important but difficult questions. Is God
known only through Christian revelation? Can man know God
through reason as well as revelation? How can specious
claims about revelation be differentiated from authentic
claims? Before long the subject of sin parades itself before
the theologian's mind. Since sin deals with man's alienation and estrangement from God, it is not long before the
subject of salvation raises its head, that is, how can man
be reconciled to God? This leads shortly to the person of
Jesus. What does Jesus do for man? Reveal God's moral will?
Redeem man? Or does he battle the forces of evil and death,
conquering them thus freeing man so that he can return to

God? Now that man has been reconciled to God the subject
of the church arises. Is it the kingdom of God in history,
or is it merely a social institution for doing good? Finally,
the end of man must be reflected upon. Is man's life simply
"a tale told by an idiot, full of sound and fury, signify-
ing nothing," or does man have the capacity for everlasting
life? These and many more are the subjects which come to
mind as the theologian begins to reflect on the Christian
story. Although they have been thought and rethought, they
must be entertained anew in our own age.

Turning our focus away from the theologian for a moment,
let us look at the creator of stories. One of the aspects
of man's nature is that he has the need to create, and much
of his creating expresses itself in art forms. Painting,
architecture, music, dance, the novel, and drama are some of
the basic expressions of art. It is through the art forms
that the spirit, values, and concerns of a particular age and
culture are expressed. A good artist then is not one who
simply copies or reproduces the subjects and the styles of
the past, but he creates or provides his own unique expression
of the spirit of his age. Hence it is not difficult for the
art historian, for example, to trace the various periods in
painting, using representative paintings to illustrate the
style exemplified in each significant stage.

Both the dramatist and the novelist are artists who
create with words rather than with colors on a canvass.

They give expression to what they see, feel, and sometimes even will. They seek to create in order to entertain, but some are revolutionaries, attempting to change the world. Often the perceptive novelist and dramatist are able, through their sensitive perception of reality, to depict or articulate what is transpiring in the soul of a nation or a whole culture. They reveal the human condition with its myriad of problems, with some going so far as to propose answers for coping with or overcoming the specific problem or condition.

The literary artist may or may not use the Christian story as the defining relationship for his existence in the world. In fact, he might well be aggressively anti-Christian. For some time now many of the better writers in the West have stood outside the Christian frame of reference. When an author is not Christian, he has some other defining relationship, and if he is a serious writer, his non-Christian commitment will be present either directly or indirectly in his works. For example, when one reads or sees Jean Paul Sartre's The Flies, Camus' The Plague, or Bertolt Brecht's The Threepenny Opera, he senses that he is encountering serious literature with a non-Christian view of the nature of reality. At the time these works were written Sartre was committed to an atheistic existentialism, Camus to a non-theistic humanism, and Brecht to Marxism. On the other hand, although their ranks continue to dwindle, there are literary artists who

are both extremely competent and committed to the Christian
faith. W. H. Auden's <u>For</u> <u>The</u> <u>Time</u> <u>Being</u> and T. S. Eliot's
<u>The</u> <u>Cocktail</u> <u>Party</u> come immediately to mind.

Knowing an author may be non-Christian or even anti-
Christian does not imply he should be censored or boycotted
by the man of faith. It simply means one ought to be perceptive and capable of making critical judgments about what
he is reading or viewing. The autonomy of the artist must
be respected, for it is from his vision of reality the
Christian is kept honest and made aware of what might be
transpiring within his own consciousness, and if not within
him, at least within the consciousness of many about him.

This leads me now to the problem of the realtionship
of theology to literature, i. e., novel and drama. How are
they to be mediated? Obviously these are separate disciplines
with the possibility of one becoming an expert within sub-
divisions of each discipline. The theologian does not wish
to have the literary artist dictating to him how to do theology, nor vice versa. In other words, I am advocating
an autonomy for the theologian and for the artist. But having
said this, the theologian may risk being a generalist and
suggests ways for relating the two disciplines to one another.
First of all, the Christian theologian comes with a prior
religious commitment, that is, he does not read a novel or
view a play in an intellectual and moral vacuum. No doubt,
his commitment will influence his evaluation of the message

of the artist. This need not imply he cannot give a high evaluation of the aesthetic aspects of an atheistic work and at the same time maintain the "answer," if one is proposed, is inadequate. In a similar way, he may well give a high rating of the "answer" of a Christian artist and a low estimate of the aesthetic aspects of the work. It is even conceivable that he may evaluate an atheistic work with respect to both its message and aesthetic quality as being superior to a Christian work with a poor articulation of its answer and inferior aesthetic achievement. Secondly, the theologian can use the artistic work as a vehicle for understanding contemporary culture. Since it is this culture he must speak to, if he is to relate the gospel meaningfully, he must know its problems, hopes, fears, and anxieties. Thirdly, he can use those few artistic works, which are Christian in message and are aesthetically adequate, as instruments for conveying the gospel to a segment of the contemporary world.

In summary, the theologian, I believe, can use the works of the modern novelist and dramatist to illustrate or express in contemporary idiom a problem for which the Christian story provides the answer, while at the same time repudiating the non-Christian answer of the author. Also, the theologian can use those artistic works which are theologically and aesthetically adequate for the apologetic purpose of expressing the Christian story to a secular world. With the relationship

of theology to literature carefully stated, I am now ready
to turn to the use of religious discourse.

2. Religious Language

For a good quarter of a century now, philosophers have
devoted a great deal of effort and debate in trying to determine what religious people are doing when they use religious
discourse. The Logical Positivists have decided it is impossible to ascertain the truth or falsity of a religious
statement; therefore, they conclude religious discourse really
is not meaningful. But not all philosophers have come to
such a frustrated dead end. R. B. Braithwaite in his well-
known essay "An Empiricist's View of the Nature of Religious
Belief"[1] has offered a plausible and (I think) valid justi-
fication for religious discourse.

Braithwaite accepts the challenge of the Logical Positivists, but he begins by agreeing with them that religious
statements are (1) not "testable by direct observation";
(2) they are not scientific hypothesis, for if they were,
they would run the risk of being refuted by experience;
(3) nor are they logically necessary, for then they could
make no factual assertions about existent reality. If
religious statements do not fall within these three areas,

---

[1]This work can be found in Philosophy of Religion, edited
by Steven M. Cahn (New York: Harper & Row, 1970), pp. 140-
163. It was originally published in 1955 by Cambridge
University Press.

then what kind of statements are they?

It is here that Braithwaite reminds us that moral discourse, though not identical with religious discourse, possesses some of the same peculiarities. For example, moral discourse is neither logically necessary, nor is it empirically verifiable, but this need not lead to the conclusion that it has no function. Obviously moral discourse has some part to play in guiding human conduct; then if it has this use, it surely has some kind of meaning. Thus, Braithwaite establishes a criterion for establishing the meaningfulness of a statement, namely "the meaning of our statement is given by the way in which it is used."[1] So the task is one of determining with the empirical method, which Braithwaite accepts, how a religious statement is used when a person engages in religious discourse to express a religious conviction.

By examining religious discourse, Braithwaite suggests the primary element in it is a moral assertion. This is to say; religious discourse reveals an attitude about what the person using it thinks is right or his duty in a particular situation. An important part of this attitude is a feeling of approval toward a specific plan of action. When a particular problem arises, it is the person's intention to act in such a way as to bring about a certain desired consequence.

---

[1]Ibid., p. 146.

Obviously Braithwaite is repudiating an emotive theory of ethics and is advocating a conative theory, that is, a moral assertion is an expression of an act of the will, rather than a simple expression of emotion. He expresses the idea as follows: "it makes the primary use of a moral assertion that of expressing the intention of the asserter to act in a particular sort of way specified in the assertation."[1] By applying the conative theory of moral discourse to religious discourse, Braithwaite develops the theory that religious discourse is conative, that is, an expression of the will. Thus, the criterion for the meaningfulness of Christian religious discourse is that it expresses the intention of the Christian to follow the Christian way of life. For instance, when the Christian asserts God is love (agape), it is encumbent upon him to follow the agapeistic way of life. The fundamental use of religious discourse is to assert one's allegiance to a set of moral principles.

Empirically, in principle, it is possible to determine whether a Christian's external actions are consistent with the commitment to love his neighbor as himself. However, Christianity not only advocates a loving external behavior; it also teaches one should have an inward loving frame of mind. When a Christian proclaims certain religious assertions, they have reference to both his internal life and his

---

[1]Ibid., p. 148.

external behavior. Once the Christian has been able to love his enemy as himself, it will not be difficult for him to act lovingly toward the enemy. Where the inner attitude has not been changed, it will be difficult to act lovingly. Although it may be possible to verify only the outer act, this does not mean there is no connection between it and the inner frame of mind.

The question obviously arises: how can religious assertions which are distinctively Christian be distinguished from those which are (for instance) Jewish? Both religions may advocate the conviction God is love and the believer ought to act lovingly toward his fellowman. Yet, there are fundamental differences between the two religions. For one thing, they observe different holy days and conduct different rituals, but Braithwaite does not think these are the most important. The fundamental difference is the two religions tell a different story or sets of stories. He defines a story as "a proposition or set of propositions which are straightforwardly empirical propositions capable of empirical test and which are thought of by the religious man in connection with his resolution to follow the way of life advocated by his religion."[1] If the Christian and the Jew act lovingly toward their fellowman, the difference which separates the one from the other is not the external act, but rather the

---

[1]Ibid., p. 155.

Christian thinks in terms of one set of stories, whereas the Jew thinks in reference to another set. Hence it is the stories the adherents of one religion tell which distinguish them from the adherents of another religion, assuming of course their moral behavior is similar.

Not only is it the different story which separates one religion from another, but it is also the story which distinguishes religious discourse from moral discourse. Of course, this does not imply that all the elements of the story must be empirically verifiable. Just as one may make reference to a novel to throw light on a point being made, one can tell or allude to the Christian story. Moral discourse as distinguished from religious discourse does not have a referrent to a particular story. Since religious discourse does, to confess one is a Christian is to assert (implicitly or explicitly) that one is able to tell the Christian doctrinal story and to commit oneself to living the Christian way of life. Without knowing the doctrinal story one would not know what was involved in committing oneself to a particular way of life. For a person to be a professing Christian then he would at the very least propose to live according to Christian moral principles and associate his intention with thinking of Christian stories.

Of course, of those who are professing Christians, there are a wide variety of opinions. The fundamentalist Christian will assert certain religious statements in the story are factual, whereas the liberal Christian will interpret them as myths, perhaps to be discarded. The neo-orthodox Christian will come along and agree and disagree with both. He might well agree with the liberal the statements are mythical, but he might disagree they must be discarded. He might even suggest they are myths, which must be interpreted in such a way, the intent of the original author be determined and then reinterpret the intent in a contemporary way. It is not my intention to settle this family quarrel, nor is it Braithwaite's. The basic point is: there is a psychological and causal connection between the story, whether it is empirically verifiable or not, and Christian behavior. Some, perhaps even most, people find it easier to decide upon and to follow through with a plan of action which might be contrary to their inclinations if this policy is associated in their minds with certain Christian stories. The story of the Good Samaritan probably never happened in the way it was told, but this fact does not detract from its ability to inform and guide moral behavior. On this point, perhaps all varieties of Christians could agree.

In order to establish my point of view further, I agree, as Braithwaite has argued, the original Logical Positivist's criterion of meaningfulness was too limited, and the use or the function of a statement must be taken into account in establishing its meaningfulness. I further agree moral assertions and religious assertions are similar, both at the primary level being conative. Although one might say more, I am willing to at least maintain being a Christian entails: (1) living according to Christian moral principles, and (2) associating this intention with seriously entertaining the Christian story or set of stories. Finally, I find it helpful to note it is possibly the story which distinguishes moral discourse from certain types of religious discourse, and it is the Christian story which differentiates the Christian from the Jew, and perhaps even from the Buddhist or Marxist. With this stated, I am ready to move to the question: why is the Christian story normative?

3. The Christian Blik

For the Christian, his story is the story. He knows there are other stories: the Buddhist, the Marxist, the Hindu, the Humanist. But he has not established a defining relationship with the other stories; his defining relationship is with the Christian story. But why has he established the defining relationship with the Christian story rather than one of the others? Perhaps, some Christians have never seriously raised this question. They have received the Christian story from their families and environment just as they have received the family inheritance. But what about the reflective Christian? He has grown up in an environment where the Christian story was normative, had for a time repudiated it, and later returned to it. He obviously is aware of other stories, and yet he has opted for the Christian story. Why?

Perhaps, R. M. Hare's explanation of a "blik" can aid us in throwing light on this problem. Quite simply a blik involves the basic presupposition by which a person orients himself, lives, and acts in the world. It is not exactly an explanation of the world, but rather, it is the presupposition which is assumed before explanation is possible. Without some kind of a blik there could be no explanation of anything. Hare states: "it is . . . true to say that . . . without a blik there can be no explanation; for it is by our bliks that we decide what is and what is not an explanation."[1]

People live by a number of bliks. The communist lives by the Marxist blik; the Buddhist lives by his particular blik, and likewise the Christian lives by his blik. To live by the Christian blik is to accept the Christian story as normative, but this does not mean some of the stories and sub-stories within the Christian story do not make some rather straightforward historical claims. This is especially the case with respect to certain assertions about the earthly career of Jesus. There is a connection, no matter how tenuous, between historical research and the faith of the Christian in Jesus because he was a historical person.

---

[1]"Theology and Falsification" in New Essays in Philosophical Theology, edited by Antony Flew and Alasdair Macintyre (London: SCM Press Ltd., 1955), p. 101.

However, accepting the Christian blik, involves more than historical statements, it is also concerned, as we said earlier, with moral statements and orienting one's self to the world in a certain way.

The reflective and self-conscious Christian, then, is aware of the other bliks, but he has not been grasped or caught up in one of them. He has been grasped by the Christian blik in the sense that he has chosen to orient his life by it. Because he lives by the Christian blik, he obviously believes it more adequately embraces the total truth than the other bliks. Otherwise he would discard it and opt for another blik. With respect to empirical existence, that is, life between the womb and the tomb, there does not appear to be a way to settle once and for all the truth of one blik over all the others. For this reason, moral and intelligent people opt for a variety of bliks. The Christian then is forced to live in a world with a plurality of bliks, which is bound to carry with this situation a degree of anxiety, risk, and uncertainty. Christians have accepted the Christian story as normative, believing it to be true, and they attempt to live their lives with this blik.

In summary, I am maintaining the Christian accepts the Christian story as his blik. He cannot necessarily prove his story is true, and another competing story is false. Not wishing to be simply an observer of life, he wants to participate in life and live. In order to do this, he must have a blik, and the Christian story fulfills this need.

4. Conclusion

I have now vaguely and cursorily established a context
and a point of view. To some, I have said too much, for I
am advocating a Christian perspective and they see no validity
in such a point of view. To others, I have not said nearly
enough. With both I must agree. For those who look only
to the wisdom of this world, the Christian story sounds
absurd. With you and with Kierkegaard, I will agree, but I
do not believe it because of its absurdity, but because it
is true in spite of its apparent absurd nature. For those
who wish that I say more, I sincerely wish that I could.
I might believe more than I can explain. But in all honesty
I do not see how one can conclusively establish the validity
of one sophisticated normative story over another with respect to life in this world. To bring in the eschatological
dimension is to beg the whole question although what is being
advocated may well be true. So I have staked out a little
intellectual plot of land on which to stand. Now I am
ready to outline some of the salient features of the normative
story.

CHAPTER II

THE ~CHRISTIAN STORY

The Christian story is the normative story for the
Christian. It represents his ultimate blik, for he has
established a defining relationship with it. It is his
norm for evaluating claims made in other stories. Because
of the importance of this story, I shall attempt to outline
briefly its salient features, and then I shall suggest a
way the Christian is more directly bound to the story.

1. The Normative Story

The Christian story is based on both the Old and the
New Testaments, and as we read the story, we immediately
sense it is a story with a plot. As with all good stories,
it has a beginning, a climax, and an end. It is a very
dramatic story, told through legends, myths, parables, and
concrete historical events. The two protagonists in the
story are God and man.

The beginning of the story is important, not because it
begins with the life of man, but rather it springs into
action before the life of any man. In fact, in the beginning,
there was not a material thing, nor man, nor animal, nor
plant, nor even light. There was only God. In the beginning
was God. This suggests there is, for lack of a better term,

19

a spiritual dimension to the universe, and the spiritual takes precedent over the material. This God was not content to be idle, but he wanted to create; so first he created the universe and later he created man.

When God had completed his act of creation, he sought to enter into direct fellowship with man (Adam). Adam, however, wanted to go his own way, rather than follow the path God had set for him. About the claim that Adam rebelled, there is general agreement, but, as to why he rebelled, there is a wide range of opinions. Reinhold Niebuhr interprets Adam's rebellion as an expression of defiant pride, of his unwillingness to obey God, whereas Harvey Cox interprets it as Adam's forfeiting his responsibility for his actions and relinquishing it to the serpent. At any rate, Adam listened to the serpent and turned his back on God. Because of this rebellion, man has been alienated and estranged from God ever since. Augustine thought the fall was a historical event, and the sin of Adam was passed on to his progeny, whereas Reinhold Niebuhr saw it as a myth depicting what all men do, namely rebel against God like a teenage son rebelling against his father. The point is the rebellion that took place in the ancient past led to a struggle between God and man and the struggle has continued to the present time.

Hardly had the alienation between God and man occurred than God took the initiative to bring about a reconciliation. As the numbers of people in the world increased, God chose

a nation of people out of all the nations of the world to be
his instrument for bringing about the desired reconciliation.
This nation was Israel, which had been given the vocation of
leading the world of rebellious people back to the creator
God. A covenant was established between these people and
God, formalizing their calling. But Israel was like Adam,
for she wanted to go her way rather than live up to the requirements of the covenant. God therefore chose a small
segment out of the nation of Israel to be his instrument for
bringing about his desired reconciliation with man. Usually
this small group of the faithful was referred to as a "remnant," but after some time God focused on a single individual
rather than a small group to initiate the reconciliation.
Isaiah spoke of the one as the "Suffering Servant." But
centuries later when the expected one did arrive, he was
thought to be none other than the son of God, the same God
who created man and the universe.

According to the Christian story, from the beginning of
creation to the birth of Jesus of Nazareth, this time period
is the "old age." It was a time in which God's relationship to man might be referred to as a "progressive reduction"
as Oscar Cullmann speaks of it.[1] The "progressive reduction"
moves from God's will for all minkind--to the people of Israel-
to the remnant of Israel--to the one who was called the

---

[1]Oscar Cullmann, Christ and Time, tr. by Floyd V. Filson
(Philadelphia: Westminster Press, MCML), p. 116.

Christ. From this perspective, we can see the Christian story is progressing along a straight line. The first part of the story moves from the act of creation by God to the anticipation of reconciliation in God's son, Jesus, who is interpreted by Christians as the Christ.

This leads us to the climax of the story which is the Christ-event. It is the Christ-event which places the whole story in proper perspective, for it is this event which enables us to understand the past, and it is this same event which throws light on the future and enables us to understand it. In fact, it is this one event which gives the whole human story its meaning. Without the mid-point of the story, which is the Christ-event, the story would be meaningless in any ultimate sense. It is the mid-point of the story that enables us to understand the whole Christian story. It provides us with the clue that enables the story to fit together in a meaningful and coherent whole.

For the Christian the Christ-event is the normative event for it is considered a revelatory event. H. Richard Niebuhr, in his work The Meaning of Revelation says:

> Revelation means for us that part of our inner history which illuminates the rest of it and which is itself intelligible. Sometimes when we read a difficult book, seeking to follow a complicated argument, we come across a luminous sentence from which we can go forward and backward and so attain some understanding of the whole. Revelation is like that . . . . The special occasion to which we appeal in the Christian church is called Jesus Christ, in whom we see the righteousness of God, his power and wisdom. But from that special occasion we also derive the concepts which make possible

the elucidation of all the events of our history.
Revelation means this intelligible event which makes
all other events intelligible.[1]

So it is the historical event beginning with the birth

of Jesus of Nazareth that provides the foundation for the

understanding of the Christian story. When religious history

is interwoven with secular history as it is in the birth of

Jesus, myth and legends are the only adequate means for trying

to express the meaning of the Christ-event. Thus, the

question whether Jesus were born of a Virgin or not is irrel-

evant, the fact that he was born is the important point.

How he was conceived is a question for the historian and

medical biologist. The story of the Virgin Birth is not

what is central, but what it is attempting to say through the

story is important, namely Jesus was the son of God. He

was God's anointed, and as such he was the instrument through

whom God was attempting to bring about a reconciliation be-

tween himself and man.

The Christ-event is larger than the sub-story about his

birth. The birth story is important in that it is the be-

ginning of the event. But it is the whole event that is

most significant, for it is concerned with Jesus' life, death,

and resurrection. All aspects must be taken together in order

to understand fully what God wished to say through the event.

In Jesus, as the Christ, God appeared in the world in

---

[1](New York: The MacMillan Co., 1941), p. 93.

a manner that he had never appeared before. God came close
to man and let him see who he is. The God who was unknown
comes and makes himself known in Jesus. In the past God
had appeared in the burning bush, in the cloud overhead,
and in many other vague sorts of ways, but in Jesus God came
to man in the form of a man. He approached man on his own
level. Without God's coming in the person of Jesus we would
not know what God was most fully like. We at the very least
know that he is personal in the sense that he cares about
persons and can enter into relationship with them.

Soren Kierkegaard illustrates the Christian claim about
Jesus in creating his own modern story, which takes on the
form of a short parable.[1] He says once there was a beautiful
humble maiden and a young handsome king. The king lived with
his wealth and in luxury in his castle; whereas the poor,
lovely maiden lived in a run down shack in the slums. In
terms of this world's goods the king had virtually everything,
whereas the poor maiden had virtually nothing. One day the
king took a ride in his horse drawn carriage, and as he passed
through the slums, he looked out into the eyes of the maiden.
It was love at first sight. The king, however, ran into a
dilemma when he returned to his castle and raised the question
about the best way to secure the humble maiden for his bride.
How could he properly convey his love and his desire to marry

---

[1]*Philosophical Fragments*, tr. by David F. Swenson (Princeton University Press, 1952), pp. 20-25.

her, a person of such a low station?

Obviously the king might take her from the low estate and raise her to his high estate, but this could smack of deception, for it might be interpreted that the king is not loving her for who she is but for whom she can become. Would the maiden be happy at the king's side surrounded by such luxury and wealth and the people at his court? Or the king could go to the maiden dressed in his official uniform, taking with him all his symbols of power, thus causing the maiden to forget herself and fall down in worshipful admiration for her sovereign. Perhaps this could even satisfy the maiden, but it would not satisfy the king because he desires the glorification of the lovely maiden rather than of himself. This is what real love demands. Finally, as the union can not satisfactorily be brought about by the elevation of the maiden, it must be brought about by descent. The king decided he must become equal with the maiden. He will appear in the likeness of the humblest, and since the humblest must serve others, the king decided he must relinquish his throne and appear in the form of a servant.

Of course, what Kierkegaard had in mind when he told the story was the Christ-event. In this story the young king represents God, and the humble maiden represents mankind. According to Kierkegaard, God comes into the human story in the form of a servant, and he reveals himself to man as a humble servant. God does this in order that the alienation between

him and his creation might be overcome, while at the same
time protecting the integrity of man, since God is a God of
love.

As the Christian tells the story, through Jesus, God
was trying to reconcile the world to himself. He was redeem-
ing mankind. He was freeing men from the fetters that bound
them to the old age and inviting them to live life freely
in the new age. He was freeing them from the fears and anxieties that held them captive. Jesus was bringing the world
back to the Heavenly Father. What Israel and the remnant
had not been able to do adequately, God was able to accomplish in the One, namely in the Christ. In fact, this event
was so decisive that Christians use it to separate the B. C.
part of the story from the A. D. part of it.

Thus far we have said that God was in the beginning of
the story and Christ is the climax of the story; so now let
us turn to the conclusion of this drama. Just as there was
a "progressive reduction" in B. C. history, there is, says
Oscar Cullmann, a "progressive advance" in A. D. history.[1]
With the Christ-event a "new age" began. Jesus gathered about
him disciples, and they went out into the world to preach
the good news about what God had accomplished in Christ.
They had experienced a reconciliation with God; so they would
share their experiences with others. As they told their

---

[1]Cullmann, op. cit., p. 117.

stories of reconciliation, others also began to experience it. New believers became a part of the new movement, until it was not long before it became a mass movement overflowing the narrow boundaries of Palestine and moving throughout the Greco-Roman world. A fellowship was started whose members were those who had experienced reconciliation; it became known as the church, the body of the One, the Christ. The church followed the instruction and the example of its Lord by moving out into the world to reconcile the world to God. This is how people through the centuries have become a part of this fellowship of reconciliation, and this is how you and I became a part of it, as it has moved through two thousand years of rugged history trying to reconcile man to the God revealed in Jesus.

So there is a "progressive advance" from the One--to the disciples--to the church--to all mankind. The Christian story then has a linear development, for it moves on a rather straight line from God in the beginning to the Christ-event at the mid-point--to God again out in the future. But this is not all there is to say, for, according to the Christian, the story has an end. Yet we must be cautious of talking about the conclusion of the story, for, as Reinhold Niebuhr has reminded us, we have overstepped our bounds when we attempt to describe the furniture of heaven and the temperature of hell. We must be cautious of such talk, for when the Biblical writers deal with these subjects, they are using mythological language.

In fact, it is not necessary for the Christian to know the details about the end of the story. The important thing is the Christian story says that there is an end, for the same God who created the universe, the God who revealed him- self in the man, Jesus, will also be present when history comes to a conclusion. Obviously the Christian story comes to an end for us the moment we die; therefore, whether the story comes to an end through the death or an individual or through an intervention of God at the end of all human stories is not all that important. The Christian claim is: when the story ends for you, God will be there.

2. Pen-Ultimate Stories

I have outlined roughly the normative story for the Christian. In this story there are sub-stories which contri- bute to an understanding and aid in the development of the plot of the normative story. The story of creation and the story about the end are examples, but the ultimate story which makes up the climax of the normative story is the Christ- event. It is ultimate in the sense that without it there would be no Christian story.

Yet there are experiences which transpire in almost every generation, nation, and even in the life of an indivi- dual which are told in narrative form. These stories are unique to those who tell them; and yet they supply a meaning within the life of an individual, nation or culture. The ancient Hebrews saw in the story of the Exodus from Egypt the mighty hand of God in history, and they used this story to give significant meaning to the Jewish story. Of course, this story is also a part of the Christian story, but it does not have the same significance for the Christian that it does for the Jew. Even a secular story such as the Bolshevik Revolution in Russia in the 1920's provides the Russian people with a way to interpret their lives and their destiny in the world.

And there are experiences within the life of an individual which he expresses in story form. It is obvious these stories are important to him. I well remember a "secular" man who viewed his four years at an Ivy League college as the most important story in his life. This story was important to him because it contained excitement, friendship, positive new experiences, and above all, meaning. Life, since college had not lived up to his expectations; in comparison it was a bitter disappointment, so he told the story of his college days over and over again. With some individuals, the story of their religious awakening is most significant. Augustine well remembered his conversion experience in the garden when he heard the voice of a child say take and read. Luther thought back on reading the passage in _Romans_ which stated the just shall live by faith alone. John Wesley, in typical English reserve, recalled how he had felt his heart strangely

warmed at a worship service in the chapel at Altersgate.
So whether religious or secular there are stories within the
life of the individual which carry significant meaning for
him.

For the Christian the normative and ultimate story is
the Christian story, but this does not mean there are no
pen-ultimate stories which are very important to him. Likewise the non-Christian or even the non-religious person may
well tell important stories about his life or nation.

3. The Normative Story and Salvation

Both the Christian and the non-Christian can tell about
the Christian story, but there is a fundamental difference
in their relationship to the story. The non-Christian tells
it as a spectator or as an objective reporter, whereas the
Christian speaks as a participant or as one existentially
related to the story. When the Christian speaks about the
reconciliation brought about between God and man in Christ,
he is not reporting about what people have said about it, but
he speaks about it from first hand experience, for he has
experienced the reconciliation. Often he will refer to that
experience as being saved. St. Paul in Romans explains carefully the dynamics of salvation, and the relationship of the
Christian to the normative story.

Just as the normative story is a story with a plot, having
a beginning, a mid-point, and an end, the experience of

salvation by the Christian is likewise a story with a plot.
Salvation concerns God and what he did in the life, death,
and resurrection of Jesus. There is a kind of objective
reality about the salvation of the Christian, for he is able
to explain exactly when and where he was saved: namely,
on the first Good Friday, at three o'clock, on a hill outside
the city of Jerusalem. So this is a part of the Christian's
experience; he turns and focuses on a past event. To be a
Christian, then, or as Paul says to be "in Christ" is first
of all to accept what happened in that past event as part of
your story. Paul says: "we were saved";[1] thus it is in faith
that we turn to the past and participate in the benefits of
the death of Christ.

But for Paul, salvation is not a static concept, for
we are not only saved, but we are in the process of being
saved. According to him, something is happening to the believer now. The Christian is "in Christ" and he is becoming
a "new creation." Love is the way we respond to the gift of
salvation in Christ as the Spirit of God works through the
believer. Not only is salvation a past event and a present
reality, but Paul says: "we shall be saved." Since the
Christian's faith and love are weak, they must be perfected.
Hope enables us to move into the future where the reconciliation begun in the Christ-event will finally be completed.

---

[1]Romans 8:24.

Hope is the way we anticipate what we are to become. Although we may not know the form or the quality of the presence beyond death, we know that God will be there.

The believer's relationship to the Christian story then involves three parts: past, present, future. The believer relates to the past in faith; he lives in the present with love, and he moves into the future with hope. Likewise, his salvation involves three stages, for he has been saved; he is being saved, and he will be saved. In all these stages there is God who is in all. God himself moves from the past into the present and out into the future.[1] To be a Christian then means to live according to Christian moral principles and to allow the Christian story or stories to inform one's life.

4. Conclusion

I have now laid out some of the important features of the Christian story. Obviously, what I have said is much too brief, for several volumes could and have been written about it. However, this skeleton will be fleshed as one of the tasks of the remainder of this essay is to explicate the Christian story in terms of stories told by the modern story teller. The important points to be emphasized are: the Christian story is not simply a story about man, but it is

---

[1] William Hamilton, "A Theology for Modern Man," in Interpretation (Oct., 1957), pp. 387-404. I am indebted to Hamilton for suggesting this interpretation of Romans.

also a story about God. In the beginning God creates; at
the mid-point, he reconciles, and at the end, he waits for
man with open arms. This story can be told objectively by a
non-believer, but the man of faith existentially appropri-
ates it in his life. When he tells the story, it is a part
of his story. He has been created by God; he has alienated
himself from God, and he has been reconciled to God through
the mediation brought about by Jesus Christ. He moves openly
out into the future knowing God will be with him.

CHAPTER III

SIN: EMPTINESS, EVIL, AND SELF-DECEPTION

In Romans, St. Paul describes the human condition.
He uses three big, general terms to characterize it. These
are sin,[1] suffering,[2] and death.[3] Having opted for the
Christian story, as did Paul, we also shall examine the
human condition from the illumination provided by these terms.
Paul says: "all have sinned and fall short the glory of God."
So we shall begin our examination of the human condition with
the category of sin. The Christian story says that Adam
rebelled against God, and his rebellion characterized him
as a sinner. What Adam did was to turn away from God and
the divine will by asserting his desire to listen to the
serpent. In other words, he turned from God who had a right-
ful claim on his life and listened to the serpent who had no
claim on him. By turning from the creator to the creature,
Adam became an idolater, for the simplest definition of
idolatry, according to Paul Tillich, is giving ultimacy to
that which is less than ultimate. Again Paul explained it
this way: "They exchanged the truth about God for a lie

---

[1] Romans 3:9.

[2] Ibid., 8:15B-23.

[3] Ibid., 5:12, 18B-21.

and worshiped and served the creature rather than the creator."

The consequence of Adam's sin is that he alienated himself from God, radically distorting his existence in the world. Rather than being a unified person, living in harmony with nature and God, he became disharmonious. He was, then, estranged from himself, nature, and God. The concept of sin is used to describe the condition or attitude of Adam after the fall. The condition or attitude precedes any specific sinful acts. The sinful act is the result of the condition in which man alienates himself from God.

The first Adam set a bad example for his progeny. They followed his lead and turned from the creator to the creature, and in so doing became sinners. Sin, however, does not simply characterize personal existence, for corporate existence is also idolatrous. The biblical writers, especially Paul and John, refer to corporate existence in terms of "this world." The world refuses to acknowledge that there is any power over it. It turns to itself, the creature, rather than acknowledging its dependence upon the Creator. So even if the Christian has been reconciled to God, he finds his existence in the world frustrating and difficult because the world which is alienated from God impinges upon him on all sides. Thus, the corporate nature of sin has rightly been called "the demonic."

From this Christian understanding of sin, we shall now examine some of the stories of modern literary artists.

These stories are told by the film artist, the dramatist, and the novelist. Many of these artists are not Christian, but their perception of the human condition is often remarkably accurate, especially when they deal with sin, though they do not use this theological term. Although their works may accurately be designated as secular, they do have an appeal to both the religious and the secular man. Thus, the theologian can legitimately use these works to establish a bridge between him and the secular man, or to translate the Christian story into a more contemporary idiom.

The prevalence of sin is ubiquitous in contemporary art forms, whether one examines a serious work like William Golding's <u>Lord</u> <u>of</u> <u>the</u> <u>Flies</u> or a popular comic strip such as Charles M. Schulz's <u>Peanuts</u>. With respect to the doctrine of sin, Schulz depicts it in terms of dirty hands. In one comic strip, Linus, a kind of philosophical questioner, is eating a sandwich in the presence of the empirical and pragmatic Lucy. Linus begins: "Hands are fascinating things! I like my hands. I think I have nice hands. My hands seem to have a lot of character. These are hands which may someday accomplish great things. These are hands which may someday do marvelous works. They may build bridges, or heal the sick, or hit home-runs, or write soul-stirring novels! These are hands which may some day change the course of destiny." Lucy looks at them and observes: "They've got jelly on them."[1]

1. Emptiness

Edward Albee's <u>Who's</u> <u>Afraid</u> <u>of</u> <u>Virginia</u> <u>Woolf?</u>[2] has
gained and held our attention for some time, for this drama
has a way of getting at people. In a church reading group,
which I once directed, we read this work. There was a woman
in the group who went out of town to a psychiatrist. Other
than her husband, I was the only one in the group to know
this. When we met at a designated member's home for our
discussion, a male member of the group immediately, in a
joking way, identified this woman with Martha. The group
went along with the designation all evening, but later the
woman informed me that the play had made such an impression
on her that she wanted to discuss it with her psychiatrist,
but he had not read it. So she took her copy to him at the
next session. What conclusions they reached I was never
told, but this experience does indicate something of the power
of the play to touch people where they live.

Albee's story begins at two in the morning with George
and Martha staggering into their living room. What the
relationship of these two characters is to our first president
and his first lady is not evident, but their names are

---

[1]Robert L. Short, <u>The Gospel According to Peanuts</u>
(Richmond: John Knox Press, 1964), p. 46.

[2](New York: Pocket Books, Inc., 1963).

George and Martha. George is forty-six and a member of the history department at New Carthage College, located in New England. Martha, George's wife, is fifty-two, and the daughter of the president of the college. They have returned from the president's home where a party was given for the new faculty members. While George prepares another drink, Martha informs him that she has invited one of the new couples over for a visit. George expresses his dissatisfaction because of the lateness of the hour and because he senses that he and his wife are on the verge of a knock-down-drag-out fight.

Shortly Nick, who is age twenty-eight and a member of the biology department, arrives with his wife, Honey, age twenty-six. Having been active in collegiate sports, Nick is in good physical condition. He also is bright, conniving, a wanting-to-get-ahead type, whereas his wife is dull, slim-hipped and puny looking. Upon their arrival, George cautions Martha not to mention the kid.

From the beginning of the first act to the conclusion of the third act, George and Martha are viciously and con-stantly at each other's throats. When they arrive home they are high, and they drink, drink, drink throughout the play. Since she makes a play for all the new men, George is certain that Martha will make a play for Nick.

As the plot develops, George refers to four games that are played throughout the play. The games are: humiliate the host, get the guests, hump the hostess, and bringing up baby. These games provide a way to organize the play through three acts of continuous drunken quarreling.

Obviously "humiliate the host" has reference to George, for he is the victim of this game. Martha releases all her fury against her husband, attempting to humiliate him in the presence of their guests. Immediately after the guests arrival, Martha goes upstairs and changes into some comfortable but very seductive clothing. As soon as George sees that she has changed, he knows exactly what she is up to, for apparently they have been through these charades many times before.

It is not long until she lets it slip they have a son who is thought to be away at school. She also is quick to opine that George has been a terrible father to his son. As the humiliation continues, she mentions a novel George wrote about a boy who accidently shot his mother and who later accidently killed his father when he swerved his automobile in order to avoid hitting an animal in the road. The result was the automobile strikes a tree and the father is dead. Martha reveals to the guests that her father would not allow one of his faculty members to publish such a ridiculous story, for it was thought such a story would ruin the reputation of his proper and conservative New England college. In defense of himself, George informed the father-in-law the story was not fiction, for it had actually happened. In fact, there was some question about whether or not this was the story of George's life. However, George yielded to the old man's demand not to publish the novel.

One might think the humiliation had gone too far, but
not to George's wife. Martha continues her onslaught by
informing the guests that when she was a young girl away at
a private school she had an affair with a gardner, but when
her father heard of it, he intervened, returning her home.
She also confesses how she had married George with the ex-
pectation he would develop his talents so that he could follow
her father as the president of the college. But Martha stresses
the fact that George is in the history department rather than
being the history department. In other words, George was a
flop and would never be president. So Martha releases all the
venom at her command because of George's shortcomings and
failings. When she has finished with her husband, he is
humiliated, if it is possible to humiliate a man who has
gone through such a ritual several times each year.

The second game is called "get the guests." At different
times during the night Nick confides bits of sensitive information about himself and Honey to George. Now the time has
come for George to pounce on his prey, for he exposes bit
by bit of what he has picked up from Nick about Honey. He
relates it as if it were a fictitious story, but containing
the correct information. Before coming to New Carthage, the
young couple had been at the University of Kansas. Apparently
there was not much of a genuine relationship between the two
although they maintained a respectable facade. As George

tells the story, Honey is so drunk and stupid she does not understand what he is doing. She therefore insists on hearing it out to the bitter end against the protestations of Nick.

As children, Honey and Nick had grown up together. Honey's father was a fundamentalist evangelist who had made a rather large sum of money in his work; thus, Nick was interested in her because of her father's savings. While they were going together, Honey had a hysterical pregnancy. Thinking she was really pregnant, Nick married her, but the truth is they have never been able to have children. So as George talks about Honey's stupidity, unattractiveness, money and false pregnancy, Nick is as humiliated as George had been earlier. As the humiliation continues, George also ridicules biology and Nick for wanting to get ahead. Had Honey the capacity for humiliation she would have been also.

As the night wears on, Honey gets sick twice. Each time she goes to the bathroom and rests on the floor. Once she rolls up like a foetus sucking her thumb and peeling the label off a brandy bottle. Her behavior, to say the least, is most embarrassing to her husband, but somewhat amusing to the devilish George.

The third game, "hump the hostess," begins when Martha reaches such a pitch she can hardly control her anger against Goerge. To retaliate, she shows more and more attention to Nick, even dancing and necking with him. Finally, at four a.m. George begins to read a book, ignoring Martha and her

philandering. While George reads, Honey sits with him as
Nick and Martha are upstairs obviously making love. Thinking she heard the doorbell ring, Honey returns to the living
room. George actually had thrown his book against the chimes,
but tells Honey a messenger has brought the tragic news that
their son has been killed in an automobile accident.

The stage is now set for the final game which is "bringing up baby." This game begins when George and Martha
start to discuss their son. Each accuses the other of being
a bad parent, of being responsible for the son never wanting
to be at home. As Martha talks tenderly about the son,
George starts to repeat the last rites in Latin. However,
Martha does not know why he is doing it, but Honey sits back
quietly with tears streaming down her cheeks. Finally,
George informs Martha their son is dead, but she denies it.
But Honey confirms it as George tells how a messenger came
with the tragic news while she was upstairs.

Again poor Honey is too dull to understand what is taking
place, but Nick senses immediately that George and Martha
have never had a child, and the story about the child is a
private game they have played with each other for years. As
the game of "bringing up baby" comes to an end, Nick and
Honey decide it is time for them to make their departure.
When they leave, George and Martha are left alone, and ironically George puts his arm around his wife as they sit peace-
fully on the living room rug.

George says: "Are you all right?"

Martha replies: "Yes. No."

George: (Puts his hand gently on her shoulder; she
         puts her head back and he sings to her, very
         softly) "Who's afraid of Virginia Woolf,
         Virginia Woolf, Virginia Woolf . . ."

Martha says: "I . . . am . . . George."

George continues his song: "Who's afraid of Virginia
         Woolf . . ."

Martha: I . . . am . . . George . . . I . . . am."[1]

The play ends on this note.

Who's Afraid of Virginia Woolf? is not a pleasant play;
it is not the kind of play we normally associate with being
a big hit. Often the general theatre public wants the kind
of drama that will entertain, that will enable them to escape from reality for an evening. Yet, they came to see
Virginia Woolf. Why? I am not sure, but it might well be
they came to alleviate their own guilt. When the play was
first produced in the early sixties, the college professor
was still placed somewhat on a pedestal, a holdover from the
fifties. Those who came to Virginia Woolf had participated
in their own version of the rituals being acted out on the
stage. They had had their drunken balls, their philandering,
and even their quarrels. They felt guilty when they did such
things, but they did not feel guilty enough to refrain from
doing them. So they went to the theatre to watch people who
were supposed to be cultured and who were thought worthy of
emulation behave in just as philistine a way as they themselves

---

[1]Ibid., pp. 241-242.

did. Very few people have the gift to quarrel the way George
and Martha do. They hit hard with their tongues, and their
quarrels make most of us look like amateurs. We therefore
can return to our homes feeling less guilty about our own
behavior, for it nowhere reaches the level of that of George
and Martha.

But what about the message Albee has for us? At one
level he is saying life is meaningless, and we must have the
courage to face this bleak fact. He depicts graphically the
emptiness of modern man; this is clearly seen in the poverty
of history as symbolized by George, the irrelevance of religion
as symbolized by the dull Honey, and the prostitution of
science as embodied in the youthful Nick. So Virginia Woolf
is a challenge to the kind of theatre we normally associate
with Broadway. It challenges the escapist musical, the
melodrama, the kind of play that maintains everything is going
to be okay.

Who's Afraid of Virginia Woolf? Who's afraid of the
big bad wolf? Who's afraid of the truth? Martha and George
had their imaginary child. We are not sure whether George's
novel was autobiographical or not. Honey had a hysterical
pregnancy and thought she heard a messenger at the door.
Truth, fantasy, and illusion are as hard to differentiate
in this story as they are in most real lives. But Albee in
a sense is challenging us to face life without illusion. To
accept it for what it is. To say that life is something that

it is not, is dishonesty. In an effort to avoid looking at the truth about herself, Martha devotes her time to tearing down George. If she were to face the truth about herself, she might not need to be so destructive toward her husband. George is a weak man, but in his relationship to Martha there seems to be the element of "I will love you, in my own perverted way, despite your defects." This is a real acceptance of the other which is the basis for developing a more positive relationship.

Even in their feeling of bitterness and in their desire to humiliate the other there is something there, for you certainly cannot say they are indifferent to each other. Indifference allows one to ignore the other, but George and Martha do not ignore. They fight, quarrel, and growl. This is not just swinging wildly, for they hit and they often hit hard. The fighting between this couple is not pretty, but it might be better than indifference. It is obviously the only kind of relationship of which they are capable.

So if we ask with George: <u>Who's Afraid of Virginia Woolf</u>, or who's afraid of the truth, Albee's #truth being to accept life as empty and ultimately meaningless, to live it without illusion, to put your arm around your spouse and accept her when she has been unfaithful to you, and even embarrassed and humiliated you, many of us might have to respond with Martha: "I ... am ... George ... I ... am."

There is little doubt that George and Martha are mythical

sons of Adam and Eve. They too have turned their backs on true being and have gone their own way. Now that they have been cast from paradise they have decided to go it alone. Their life style reveals the emptiness of such an existence. In their meaningless world, they can only humiliate and then place their cold arms around each other and endure. Yet their acceptance of one another is still empty as symbolized by Martha's barrenness in being unable to conceive a child.

Albee's drama is powerful, for it does depict vividly the human condition in a godless universe, and there is an attractiveness about the way he pursues the truth. Even his indirect criticism of Honey's evangelistic father has merit. But if the Christian story is the norm, then the story of Virginia Woolf only depicts the human condition of man as sinner; its message of simple acceptance of this condition and human endurance is not enough. The Christian story says that man is not only a sinner, but he can be changed. This change cannot take place simply by willing it. It must come from outside himself. The power to change is there if George and Martha will only seek it out in the right place.

2. Evil

As we continue our examination of the human condition through literary works, we shall examine John Whiting's The Devils.[1] Whiting was an English playwright, and Peter

---

[1](New York: Hill and Wang, 1961).

Hall said of him that he was "a man born to be unlucky."[1]
During his relatively short life he knew little success.
The Devils opened in London in 1961 and received excellent
reviews as well as having a successful run. It came to this
country in the mid-sixties, but before it arrived Whiting had
died in 1962 at the age of forty-five. Some considered The
Devils the author's breakthrough, but he died too soon for
this to be certain.

So let us look at the story Whiting tells in this drama.
With the exception of a short scene, the action takes place
in or around Loudun in France between the years 1623-1634.
The plot of the play centers around two people who inciden-
tally do not even meet each other until the very end of the
play. One of the characters is a priest, Grandier, who is
the vicar of St. Peter's Church in Loudun. The other character is Sister Jeanne of the Angels, who is the prioress of
St. Ursula's Convent. In the American production Jason
Robards played the part of the priest and Anne Bancroft played
that of the nun.

The style of the drama is conventional. There are three
acts, and the play opens with an eighteen year old man hanging
from a gallows. We soon learn the young man had been in love
and had stolen to buy for his beloved. In other words this
was his crime. As the worshippers file out of the church,

---

[1] Peter Hall, "A Man Born to be Unlucky?" New York Times,
November 14, 1965.

they see the criminal hanging from the gallows; but their conversation is either about the priest, Grandier, or his sermons. The doctor and the chemist are in the crowd, and they are the stereotyped solid citizens. As a young widow leaves the church, they remark that she has overcome the death of her husband very well. They were confident that her ability to cope with her bereavement was due more to the private visits of the priest than to his sermons. In other words, they were certain that Grandier was carrying on a clandestine affair with the rich widow. The governor of Loudun also leaves the church with a town official. He expresses concern about Grandier's sermon, for he sees disturbing political implications in the priest's remarks. Finally, Grandier himself comes out of the church, and the sewerman throws a shovel of filth on the priest's garments, but the priest is not offended.

We sense almost immediately that Grandier is a man with great ability; he is learned, sensitive, and culturally polished. Yet, behind all these talents, there lies hidden a very complex personality. In a later scene the governor tells one of his officials about observing the priest. The governor says: "Grandier came to see me this morning. I was having breakfast in the garden. He didn't know that I could observe him as he walked toward me. Vulnerable: smiling. He visibly breathed the air. He stopped to watch the peacocks. He fondled a rose as if it were the secret part of a woman.

He laughed with the gardener's child. Then he composed himself, and it was another man who sat beside me and talked
for an hour. Where will this other man climb on his ladder
of doubt and laughter?"

The governor's listener replies: "Probably to the
highest offices of the church."

Then the governor asked: "And the man I saw in the
garden?" (There was silence.)[1]

As the plot unfolds, we discover that the rumors about
Grandier are not false. The priest is carrying on an affair
with a rich, young widow. Later he meets with the daughter
of the town prosecutor, and is asked to provide the young
lady with lessons in Latin. Each week Grandier meets with the
daughter and the expected happens; they fall in love. So
Grandier and Phillipe perform their own private wedding
ceremony, but again the inevitable happens. Phillipe becomes
pregnant, and Grandier instructs her that she must tell her
father everything and request that he secure a good man for
her to marry.

Not only are things beginning to happen in town, but
there is also action in the convent. The priest-director
of the convent, who is an old man, dies, thus creating a need
for his replacement. Sister Jeanne, a very emotionally
disturbed person, is responsible for securing a new director.

Whiting, op cit., p. 14.

The sister's appearance is unusual in that she has an ugly
hump on her back, which she interprets as her cross to bear.
Although she seeks to repress it, she has a very strong erotic
drive. Her prayers are very revealing of her erotic nature.
In one of them she is praying to Jesus and says: (silence)
"Mercy." (silence) "I will find a way. Yes, I will find a
way to You. I shall come. You will enfold me in your sacred
arms. The blood will flow between us, uniting us. My innocence is Yours."[1]

As with everyone in Loudun, Sister Jeanne has heard of
the libertine priest, Grandier, and she and the other women
of the convent feel it is God's will they invite him to become their director. When Grandier receives the letter of
invitation, he politely refuses the position.

Following the refusal by Grandier, Sister Jeanne and
several other nuns feel they have been possessed by demons;
and the power over the demons is controlled by the libertine
priest. The women have all kinds of erotic fantasies. At
times they speak with masculine voices; they have visions of
being raped, and Sister Jeanne has a hysterical pregnancy.
Yet, upon careful examination by the bishop's physician,
the women still possess the signs of their virtue. However,
there is a very crude scene in which the local doctor and the
chemist attempt to free the nun of her demon possession.

_____

[1]Ibid., p. 29.

They, knowing of Grandier's other activities, feel that in some way he is responsible for the demon possession of the nuns.

On one occasion when the women are going through one of their fits caused by the demons, a prince, representing the king of France, comes and observes. After they have passed through the bizarre antics of their possession, the prince informs them he has a container with some of the original blood of the Savior in it. The prince asks one of the priests if the blood could cure the women of their possession; he assures him that it could. Hence, as the container is passed ceremoniously over the women, they regain their composure; they twist their mouths as if the demons were making their exits by way of the oral cavity. After the women have returned to normal, the prince then informs them the container was empty, opening it and allowing them to examine it. He bluntly informs them their possession is a fraud.

The less successful priests in Loudun are jealous of Grandier, for many of their parishioners have been attending services at St. Peter's because they like the controversial priest. These jealous priests join in a conspiracy with the doctor and the chemist to assure the nuns they most certainly have been possessed by demons, and the demons will return to possess them again. In fact, if the demons do not return, this will throw into question the integrity of the nuns about the first possession. If the nuns were merely charading, their eternal souls might well be in danger. So with a little coaxing, the women are frothing at the bit again, accusing Grandier of being responsible for the possession.

Meanwhile, out in the town the plot continues to thicken. The trouble there tends to be more political, for Cardinal Richelieu has persuaded Louis XIII, the king of France, that the nation should be unified. The citizens should come to feel they are citizens of France rather than just members of their local communities. Thus, the Cardinal encourages the king to demand that the walls of Loudun be torn down. The king's representative comes to the governor of Loudun trying to persuade him to tear the walls of the town down, whereas Grandier sides with the governor encouraging him to withstand the pressure. So word of Grandier's obstinate political activity reaches the royal court. For a short time the king wavers on the question about the walls, but Richelieu assures him it is the proper course of action. This places Grandier on a collision course with the cardinal and king; hence they feel the priest must be eliminated. With this in mind, the king sends an investigator to secure the necessary evidence for convicting Grandier of some major crime.

Shortly, a meeting of the Council of State is convened to evaluate the evidence against Grandier. Among those present are the king's investigator, who was responsible for obtaining the necessary evidence for a conviction, and the prince, who had exposed the fraud of the nuns' demon possession. When

the investigator presents his evidence against Grandier, he
maintains the priest is responsible for the demon possession,
and the possession is genuine. Furthermore, he claims
Grandier's living quarters have been examined and manuscripts
were found showing the priest's criticisms of the Royal
Court and supporting the governor's position of maintaining
the fortifications around Loudun. Finally, he reveals there
was evidence Grandier had been in love with a woman, and the
priest had engaged in several amorous affairs with women.

The prince shows his disgust with the manner of convicting Grandier. He points out that the priest is innocent
of the charges of being responsible for the demon possession,
which is the major indictment. The prince says: "For the
love of Jesus Christ, if you wish to destroy the man, then
destroy him. I'm not here to plead for his life. But your
methods are shameful. He deserves better. Any man does.
Kill him with power, but don't pilfer his house, and hold
evidence of this sort against him. What man could face
arraignment on the idiocy of youth, old love letters, and the
pathetic objects stuffed in drawers or at the bottom of
cupboards, kept for the fear that one day he would need to
be reminded that he was once loved? No. Destroy the man
for his opposition, his strength or his majesty. But not for
this!"[1]

---

[1]Ibid., p. 93.

The inevitable happens; Grandier is unanimously found guilty of being a man of the devil. Hence he is held accountable for the demon possession. His penalty is that he will be burned at the stake for his sins.

As he is prepared for execution, Grandier reminds us somewhat of the preparations made two thousand years earlier. His head is shaven, and he is taken into a back room, where he is informed that his torture will be lighter if he will confess his guilt. Of course, he maintains he is innocent of the crimes he has been accused of committing. He is not responsible for the demon possession. As a means of trying to persuade him of his guilt, both legs are cruelly broken with large hammers. But again he maintains his innocence, so his tormentors argue the devil is aiding him by preventing the torture from being fully felt.

By the time Grandier is removed from the torture chamber and dragged through the streets of Loudun, over thirty thousand people have gathered for the public execution, many of them coming from neighboring villages. As the criminal is dragged through the streets, the procession passes the gate of the convent, and for the first time the accused meets the accuser. The priest Grandier meets the nun, Sister Jeanne. At this moment the executioners ask him to admit his guilt for the demon possession and seek the nun's pardon, but he proclaims his innocence, insisting he has never seen the nun before. Grandier is then taken to the stake where he is torturously burned.

Following the execution, Phillipe, Grandier's young lover
who is now enormously pregnant, returns home with an old man
to whom she has been married. Sister Jeanne walks through
the streets where she meets the sewerman. As they are talking
people are sifting through the ashes in order to obtain pieces
of Grandier's remains. The sewerman picks up a piece and
hands it to Sister Jeanne, but she refuses to accept it.
She walks away and screams: "Grandier! Grandier!" There
is an empty silence, which is broken by the falling curtain.

The story of The Devils is a story about man's evil,
and in it Whiting repudiates any pollyanna optimism that
says all is right with the world. In this story evil is
victorious in bringing about the death of Grandier; but in
the face of evil the priest was still able to endure, for to
the very end he refused to accept the guilt for something
for which he was not guilty. So, on the one hand, we find
the ugly, the destructive, the cruel, and the demonic, and,
on the other hand, we see the ability to endure and maintain
one's integrity to the very end.

In this story evil is ubiquitous. It is exemplified
in the solid citizens' pious morality. The chemist and the
doctor are superficially religious men, but underneath they
are ruthlessly immoral. When they approach Grandier's bishop
with their accusations, he sees right through them. He says:
"I'll accept your reasonable intentions in coming here.

Although, God knows, if there's any one I distrust it's
the good citizen going about his civic duty. His motive is
usually hate or money. But I will not accept your opinions,
your advice, nor, for a moment longer, your presence."[1]

Evil is present in the political fabric of Grandier's
society, as seen in the Royal Court. Obviously the king had
the power to eliminate the priest on the basis of their dis-
agreements. Grandier thought the fortifications should remain around Loudun, but the king and his cardinal thought
otherwise. But they refused to eliminate Grandier for
treason; instead they allowed the uninformed public to dispose
of him on the erroneous grounds of demon possession. Along
these lines, Albert Camus, in his novel, The Stranger, reminds
us that often men are not executed for the crimes they have
committed but for some other reason. The Stranger was convicted not because of his killing of a man in self-defense,
but because he did not cry at his mother's funeral. Likewise, Grandier did not die because of his libertine immorality,
nor because of his political views, but because of a trumped-
up charge of demon possession.

Several forces came together to destroy Grandier. The
Royal Court wanted him out of the way for political reasons.
The doctor and the chemist desired his destruction because
they disagreed with his morality. The other priests wanted

---

[1]Ibid., p. 40.

him done away with because they were envious of his superior ability, and their parishioners were attending his services rather than theirs. A group of frustrated, neurotic women provided the vehicle through which all these evil forces could work in order to destroy Grandier.

In addition to evil, Whiting also touches on the problem of faith and doubt. Just before Grandier was arrested, he thought his faith was strong, for he had confidently sat at the bedside of an old man who had just died. But as the priest experienced the torture, which would bring about his own death, would he be able to maintain his faith? The Commissioner touched on the problem in this way: ". . . but when you are stretched out in that little room, with the pain screaming through you like a voice, let me tell you what you will think. First: how can man do this to man? Then: how can God allow it? Then: there can be no God. Then: there is no God. The voice of pain will grow stronger and your resolution will grow weaker. Despair, Grandier. You used the word yourself. You called it the gravest sin. Don't reject God at this moment. Reconcile yourself. For you have bitterly offended Him. Confess."[1]

If in maintaining his innocence, he kept his faith, then Grandier retained his faith. But it is ambiguous whether or not he kept his faith in God. We do know, however, the

---

[1]Ibid., p. 114.

play ends on a note of human passion, rather than on a direct
affirmation of God. As I mentioned above, Sister Jeanne
at the end does not cry out to God, but she screams:
"Grandier! Grandier!" But there is no Grandier, for the
devils have destroyed him.

As with <u>Virginia</u> <u>Woolf</u>, <u>The</u> <u>Devils</u> is a powerful story
depicting aspects of the human condition, especially the
corporate nature of sin. George and Martha lived a type of
existence in which they had turned their backs on the Creator,
and the society of Loudun likewise had done the same thing,
despite its protestations to the contrary. With the society
alienated from its source of being, sin became corporate,
manifesting itself through the evil permeating the institutions of society. These include the political structure as
expressed through the King and Royal Court, the scientific
community as seen in the doctor and the chemist, the common
man, and even the religious institution as exemplified in
the Cardinal and the envious priests. Whether Grandier was
a man reconciled to his Creator, or whether he simply was of
strong integrity, the point is: he was frustrated by evil
and was ultimately destroyed by it.

It is not too difficult to view Grandier's destruction
from the background of the ultimate destruction of Jesus.
Many of the same forces which brought about the crucifixion
also led to the burning at the stake. With Grandier, however,
it is not easy to determine how strong his integrity was.

The problem is that once he was found guilty he was going to die at the stake. There is no indication that his willingness to admit his guilt and repent would save him. Of course, his admittance would have diminished the amount of torture, so there is the clear indication that he was a man of some integrity, for he refused the offer of leniency.

In any case, Grandier's integrity can be appreciated by the Christian. Obviously there is some sense in which the Christian story is or has informed Grandier's autobiography. If his integrity was predicated on his faith in God as revealed in the Christian story, then the connection with reconciliation is more obvious. However, even then, there are parts of Grandier's life style which many Christians would find objectionable, so this leads to further questions about what evaluation might be made about the priest. It might well be that he was a man of God whose faith and love needed to be perfected.

Whiting's story should not be viewed as a historical drama based simply on Aldous Huxley's The Devils of Loudun. It is that, but the author is speaking about the world in which you and I live. In other words, if we follow the example of the one who made our reconciliation possible, we too will run the risk of being frustrated and possibly even taken to some modern version of the stake. Sin has incarnated itself as firmly in our contemporary institutions as it did in Loudun. Whiting, though using a different idiom, is reminding us of this fact, which we would do well not to take lightly.

3. Self-Deception

Gabriel Marcel was both an existentialist and a Roman
Catholic. He presented his views of the human condition
in both technical philosophical works and in drama. As was
the case with Virginia Woolf, his plays tend to be rather
personal, dealing with the family, especially as the members
interact with each other. His four act play, A Man of God,
reveals vividly his understanding of the human condition.[1]

A Man of God has a simple plot and contains very little
action. Its basic strength, it seems to me, lies in Marcel's
ability to peel off each layer of his character's personality
somewhat the way a housewife takes off the layers of an
onion, the self is exposed in all its nakedness. The setting
for this play is an apartment in Paris, the home of a Protestant clergyman and his family. Claude Lemoyne is the
minister, who lives with his wife, Edmee, and his daughter,
Osmonde. The action begins when the minister and his wife
begin to notice that their daughter is showing more than a
casual interest in a man who lives in the apartment above
them. The man's wife has had a psychotic breakdown, and he
now lives alone with his two small children. The doctor's
prognosis is that the wife will never recover. Thus, Osmonde,

---

[1]Three Plays (New York: Hill and Wang, 1958), tr. by
Rosalind Heywood.

the minister's daughter, shows more than a passing interest
in the small children, even babysitting for them in order to
be near the father.

Claude's mother has been visiting with the family, and
Francis, Claude's brother and a local physician, comes for
the mother so that she can visit with his family. During the
conversation between Claude and Francis we learn that the
doctor has recently examined a male patient who has only a
very short time to live. The patient is a former lover of
Edmee's and is in fact the father of Osmonde. Shortly after
Edmee's marriage to Claude, she had an affair with this man,
and he even wanted them to go away together, but she refused
to leave Claude although she was in love with the man.
Apparently she considered life with her lover too much of
a risk; therefore, she returned to Claude who was at the time
having trouble with his parish and who also had an unfortunate
experience in a counselling situation. When Edmee returned
to her husband, she confessed her unfaithfulness to him.

Having problems at home and in his vocation, Claude's
back was to the wall. In fact, he was experiencing an emotional crisis. However, it was through his failure in the
parish, in his counselling, and in his marriage, that he had
what he interpreted to be a genuine religious experience.
The result was that he was able to forgive his wife and remain
in the ministry. Since this early crisis, Claude had been
very successful, moving from one good church to a better one.

On the surface, he was a man who truly lived his faith, and he was thought to be very forgiving, too good, and too generous. People felt he did a lot of good for his parish.

With the re-appearance of the dying lover on the scene, Claude felt this was a time for genuine testing. As the man wanted to come to the Leymones to see his daughter, Claude agreed that he should come like any other visitor. So against Edmee's strong protest, Claude allows the dying man to visit. Shortly after the arrival of the visitor, Claude is forced to leave for an important meeting, so that Edmee and her former lover are left alone. They talk about the past, and the lover accuses Edmee of being a coward; for she had confessed their affair to Claude because she was afraid to risk life with him. He tries to convince her that she is partly responsible for his mortal condition in that he turned to a wild life after she left him, and now the results of such physical abuse were killing him.

As the story develops, we see layer after layer of Claude's personality peeled off, and we begin to view him from a different perspective. In fact, it is not simply that we come to see him differently, but he comes to perceive himself in a radically new way. Rather than being in the ministry because he chose to be there, Claude was driven into the ministry by his over-zealous mother. She had praised him when he considered it, and she withdrew her praise when he considered another vocation. He came to believe he might have been a better businessman, but his parents would not allow it.

Furthermore, he discovers, much to his surprise, the reason he was able to forgive his wife for her infidelity was that he really did not love her fully. He loved her only in some distorted, vague, Christian sense in which a man of faith ought to love his fellowman, but he did not love her physically as a woman which she not only desired but needed. Also, he had gone through the act of forgiveness because he did not wish to cause a public scandal which would have wrecked his ministerial career. So rather than being the authentic Christian minister who forgave his wayward wife, he had forgiven her because it really had not cost him anything, and besides it paid its dividends. She provided someone for him or practice his perverted form of Christian charity upon.

Although Edmee had been unfaithful, with several members of the family knowing about it, she had maintained a good front for Claude. Being active in church and civic affairs, she was actually going through the motions of being good, but there did not appear to be any love or involvement in what she was doing. She was almost unconscious of her acts of kindness.

In the midst of this time of testing for Claude, Osmonde confesses to her father that she has many doubts about life, that she is not a person of religious faith. She even discloses to him that their whole life together as a family

has appeared to her as superficial and meaningless. She
also cinfides that she is going away with the man and his
two children, which means she has decided to take care of the
children and be the man's mistress. With Osmonde expressing
herself with all candor, Claude decides to do the same.
Not wanting to cause unnecessary suffering to his daughter,
nor wishing to cause himself the discomfort, Claude had
refrained in the past from telling Osmonde that she was not
his daughter. Now he tells her.

As the story of the Lemoynes comes to an end, Claude
has realized his devious motivations and discovers within
himself strong feelings of hostility which had been repressed.
He informs his mother that it was she who forced him into the
ministry. She shrugs it off by telling him that he is being
considered for a larger and more prestigious church, but he
confesses to her that he is now spiritually bankrupt.
Osmonde knows now that Claude is not her father, and she is
going away with her married lover without any illusions as
to what she is getting into. It appears as if Claude is going
to leave Edmee and have her go to her dying lover. He even
suggests she might commit suicide with him, but she is not
willing. Although Claude will go on living, he thinks he is
leaving the ministry.

At the very last minute a parishioner and her little
son stop by the apartment. The parishioner tells Claude what
a good man he is, and about the great amount of good he has

done for other people. After the parishioner has departed, Edmee tells Claude they have to go on living; he had to maintain his vocation, for his people were receiving benefits from his ministry. But Claude turns over and over again in his mind the idea: "to be known as one is."

In order to understand more clearly Claude's journey toward self-discovery, I should like to refer to three comments made in the course of the play. First, when speaking with his brother, Francis, Claude says: "If my life was based on sham, it was far better to expose it ... You live for years with a certain idea of yourself, and you think you are drawing strength from that idea. Then suddenly you're living in a fool's paradise ... What I mean is that when I look back on the past, the things I used to say and think have become meaningless."[1]

Second, when speaking to his wife, Edmee, he says: "When I forgave you I thought it was an act of Christian charity. But apparently I was simply running away from scandal and loneliness. It was you who forced me to open my eyes."[2]

Third, in a conversation with his daughter, Osmonde, he says: "I've had enough of being humiliated and trampled on. It's my turn to hurt somebody." Osmonde replies:

---

[1] Ibid., p. 81.

[2] Ibid., p. 83.

"you---couldn't." Claude responds: "Oh, yes I could. I
could now---hurt them, knock them about, throw them out of
the house ... So this is what I have come to. It's like
drunk. For the last two days it has been boiling up inside
me--feelings I have never had before, the words I had never
said ... It's terrifying! Just now I found myself talking
aloud to myself. If you'd heard the things I was saying!
It can't go on. Tell me it won't go on ... No, no, don't
tell me that. I'm not sure that I want it to stop."[1]

As we examine Marcel's story, we immediately perceive the
complexity of human behavior and human motivation. The author
is pointing out to us that in the good there is the bad, and
in the bad there is the good. Life seldom presents itself in
either/or alternatives. This makes being human much more
difficult to understand and pass judgment on. Claude on the
surface appeared as an ideal Christian, but below the surface
his motivations were far from altruistic. They basically
were selfish. So with Claude, who appeared to be a good
man, there was the bad. Yet at the time he did not even know
he was bad. On the other hand, Edmee, who appeared to Francis and Osmonde as bad, did acts that were good. Although her
good was entangled with the bad, there is an element of good
in the bad Edmee. She does enable Claude to come to his new
self-awareness, and she does acts of charity even if for the

---

[1]Ibid., p. 104.

wrong reasons. Thus, in a sense Claude was the bad-good husband, and Edmee was the good-bad wife. Both people were complicated, with each's behavior entangled with both good and
bad.

Marcel is also reminding us that the human condition is
plagued by self-deception. We live, not in a real world, but
in an illusory one. We have a misconception of ourselves,
and consequently we misunderstand others. We are often strangers to ourselves, just as Claude was. Our estrangement,
not only affects us, but it affects others, for we confuse
and bring misery to others. Claude, who could not love
Edmee as a man ought to love his wife brings misery to her.
Edmee who could not risk a life with her lover brought misery
to him. The lover by telling Edmee that she was responsible
for causing him to abuse himself caused her to suffer. And
Osmonde, who has suffered because of these three, makes
Claude and Edmee suffer by going away with the married man.
Thus, Marcel is maintaining that to refuse to recognize the
bad and evil in ourselves is to live a life of self-deception.

For Marcel, our self-deception has to be exposed. We
have to view ourselves immediately as we really are, and this
is not easy, for we need our illusions and deceptions at one
time or another. We need them about ourselves and our abili-
ties, so it is painful to have our cherished balloons busted.
But this is what is necessary, if man is to attain a higher
level of existence. Once we have reached this higher level

of awareness then we are in a position to see that man is more
than what he immediately appears to be. There is an element
of "Mystery" about his existence, and one must open himself
to the "Mystery" if he is to overcome the despair and emptiness which almost always follows the casting away of self-
deception. Claude has rid himself of self-deception, and he
is now in a state of despair. This is where Marcel leaves
him, but in his philosophy, there is the possibility of
Claude now opening himself to the "Mystery" and attaining
authentic being.

As the play ends, Claude, Edmee, and Osmonde are going
to go on living. They are going to attempt to face life
without self-deception or illusions. Obviously they can no
longer live with their old deceptions, for they have been
exposed. Whether they will create new deceptions or open
themselves to the surrounding "Mystery," we do not know.
But both are possibilities that now open to them.

4. Conclusion

Since the mythical time of Adam and Eve, man and woman
have been cast from earthly paradise. As the offspring
of this primal couple, we are all in a state of alienation.
The three plays we have just considered throw light on the
kind of existence people experience outside of Eden. Both
Albee and Marcel reveal how we are estranged from ourselves
and others. In this state, we create our self-deceptions.

Both challenge us to turn away from these crippling illusions and see the human condition for what it is. It is plagued by emptiness and meaninglessness. Whereas Albee's vision offers no relief from the condition, Marcel's does. All three plays touch on man's evil, that is, his ability to cause others to suffer. Albee and Marcel point out the interpersonal dimension of this problem, whereas Whiting focuses on the social dimension in which the institutions of society are permeated with evil. So whether we speak about man at the personal or the social level, we come immediately upon that aspect of the human condition which in Christian terminology is called sin.

CHAPTER IV

SIN: MURDER, PARADOX, AND SILENCE

Three aspects of the human condition, which were forcefully touched on in the nineteen sixties, were murder, para-
sox, and silence. These aspects were vividly illustrated in
the works of Truman Capote, Friedrich Durrenmatt, and Rolf
Hochhuth. So as we attempt to further our analysis of the
human condition under the rubric of sin, we shall examine
a work by each of these authors.

1. Murder

According to the Christian story, after Adam and Eve
rebelled against the Creator, they were driven from the
Garden of Eden. In time they had two sons. The older was
called Cain and the younger was named Abel. These sons
were conceived outside the original paradise; hence, they
were born and grew up in a state of alienation from their
Heavenly Creator. When they were adults, Cain became a farmer
and harvested grain. Abel, however, became a shepherd and
raised sheep. In trying to overcome their separation from
God, Cain offered a sacrifice of grain, whereas Abel offered
a lamb. Apparently God detected a lack of sincerity in Cain
and was displeased with his offering; however, he knew that
Abel had presented his offering with the utmost sincerity.

Cain, sensing God's displeasure, developed a bad case of
sibling rivalry. He was overcome with a seige of jealousy,
and in this blinding state went out into the field with his
brother, Abel. An argument ensued, and the older brother
rose up and killed his younger brother. With this dastardly
act, murder entered the world. So the simple act of dis-
obedience on the part of the parents led to murder in the
children.

Once murder entered the world many followed the example
of Cain. Ugly stories about murder have been told again and
again since that early time. In the mid-nineteen-sixties,
the American writer, Truman Capote, told one such story
in his work, In Cold Blood.[1] At the time the work appeared,
much attention was given to it in the literary magazines,
for Capote maintained he was offering a new literary form.
He called it the "non-fiction novel," and he offered his book
as an example of the new literary form. Although the theory
of the non-fiction novel is worth considering, we shall be
concerned only with the story.

The setting for In Cold Blood is Holcomb, a town with
about two-hundred-seventy inhabitants, located in western
Kansas. The time is mid-November of nineteen-fifty-nine.
Since the story reads like a well developed murder mystery
there must be victims. In this case the victims were the

---

[1] (New York: Random House, 1965).

Herbert Clutter family. The Clutters were well-to-do farmers living just outside Holcomb. Mr. Clutter was an honest, hard-working man. He was an active Methodist, and he voted Republican. He neither smoked nor drank. He paid his hired help well, and he was a highly respected member of the community.

The Clutters had three daughters. One daughter had married and moved away from Holcomb. Another daughter was away at school, and she was engaged to be married shortly. Nancy, the youngest daughter, was sixteen and still living at home. Since she was the only physically well female at home, most of the chores around the house fell to her. Although she did most of the cooking and cleaning at home, she was still a very good high school student. In a sense, she was the all-sufficient small town girl, for she had looks and charm, and she did everything well.

In the case of Mrs. Clutter, things were not so well. For several years she had been plagued by various kinds of emotional problems. Sometimes her problems were so great that she had to be hospitalized. So through the years she had withdrawn to her room, allowing the other members of the family to run the house.

Kenyon was the only son. He tended to be rather quiet, with his main enjoyment being his own private workshop. And he too was a good student. Whereas Nancy was outgoing like her well-liked father, Kenyon was more shy and withdrawn like his mother. If Holcomb had chosen a family to be the all-American family, it no doubt would have chosen the Clutters.

However, on the night of November 14, 1959, Perry Smith and Richard Hickock drove to the Clutter farm. With a twelve gauge shot-gun and a hunting knife, they entered the Clutter home. They took Mr. Clutter and tied him in the basement, allowing him to lie comfortably on a mattress carton. Likewise they took Kenyon to the basement, securely tied him on an old couch, and placed a pillow under his head, so that he too might be comfortable. Nancy was tied in her bed, with the covers placed carefully over her so as to protect her modesty. Mrs. Clutter also was tied in her bed. After Smith and Hickock had carefully gone through the house looking for money, they returned to the basement. Smith cut Mr. Clutter's throat, and then at close range shot him. He then shot Kenyon and went upstairs and used his twelve gauge shot-gun on Nancy and Mrs. Clutter.

When the Clutters were discovered, the little town of Holcomb went into a state of shock. Various members of the community had their theories about who and why this all-American family was murdered, but none of them could be substantiated. Although the townspeople had lived together for years, they were afraid and distrustful of one another until the case was finally solved.

After committing this terrible tragedy, Perry Smith and

Richard Hickock returned to a small town near Kansas City where Hickock's poor farming parents lived. Within a week following the murders, Hickock and Smith passed off over seventy bad checks in Kansas City and then left for Mexico, they thought, for good. But they spent all their money and even had to sell their automobile, so they returned to the States, even to Kansas City, where they stole an automobile and passed several other bad checks. They drove to Miami for the Christmas vacation, and after a few days bathing in the sun, they decided to return West again. On January 2, 1960, they were picked up in Las Vegas, they thought, for violating a parole and for passing bad checks. In less than two months after the infamous murders, they were captured.

When Smith and Hickock made their exit from the Clutter home, they had left some footprints in the basement which, though not visible to the normal eye, were picked up by a sensitive camera. Also, they had taken from Kenyon's room a portable Zenith radio which was missed by the cleaning woman. Other than these two clues, very little evidence linking them to the Clutter premises was possible.

But even these two clues were not enough for the detectives to go on. There had to be something else. As fate would have it, a prisoner in the Kansas State Penitentiary at Lansing read about the murders in the newspaper and heard about them on the radio. The prisoner, Floyd Wells, had been a cellmate with Richard Hickock, and about ten years earlier had worked on the Clutter farm. Wells had told Hickock about the Clutters, e. g. their wealth, how the house was laid out, and their habits. In talking about his past employer, Wells had even lied, for he had told the eagerly listening Hickock that Clutter had a safe in his home with a large sum of money in it. However, the truth was that Mr. Clutter was the kind of man who kept very little cash at home and did all his business by check, even writing one for his haircut. So when Floyd Wells heard about the Clutter story, he knew that Hickock was involved because the crime had gone about the way Hickock had planned it while in prison. Since there was a reward and the possibility of receiving a shortened sentence, Wells went immediately to the Warden with his story. This provided the essential lead that was needed.

Later Kenyon's radio was discovered in a hock shop in Mexico City, and the shoes, which were worn by Smith, were also found. The shot-gun and knife were later found at Hickock's parents farm, and the left-over rope and tape were found buried on the Clutter farm. When confronted with the evidence, both Smith and Hickock confessed their involvement in the crime.

According to Capote, the fundamental motive for the crime was robbery. Hickock had planned everything, even the killing of the family. Although Smith had originally gone along for the money, Hickock had actually manipulated him so that Smith did the actual killing. Moreover, Capote thinks that

Hickock had an abnormal attraction for young girls, and had every intention of sexually assaulting Nancy, but Smith would not allow it.

In any case the judicial system moved along its normal course, and the trial was held in Garden City, a town near Holcomb. Both Smith and Hickock were found guilty and scheduled for the gallows at one minute past midnight on Friday 13, 1960. With the standard legal maneuvers and appeals, their appointment with the hangman was postponed. Finally they were hanged at the Kansas State Prison on April 14, 1965. Hickock was age thirty-three and Smith was thirty-six.

When we consider a crime of this nature, we become interested in the backgrounds of the criminals. Richard Hickock was the son of a poor farming family who resided outside a small Kansas town. He had an intelligence quotient of one-hundred-thirty, and he had been a relatively good student and an even better athlete. He would have liked to have gone to college, but felt he could not make it financially. When he was nineteen, he married a girl sixteen, but this marriage ended in divorce. Later, he married a lover whom he also divorced. Although two children were born during his first marriage, he did not have any in the second marriage. At one time he received a slight brain concussion as the result of an automobile accident. Later, he served a prison sentence for passing bad checks. Capote portrays Hickock as a wild, mean punk, who thought he was smarter than most men and intended to take advantage of them. Yet, he could not kill although he could plan the details of a murder if some-one else would actually carry them out.

As to Perry Smith, he was the son of a Cherokee mother and an Irish father. His parents had been a riding-stunt team for a rodeo; hence, they were always on the move, making it impossible for their children to receive an adequate education. After the Smiths had to give up their career as entertainers, they were divorced. The mother had always been promiscuous, and later she became an alcoholic, dying one night in her own drunken vomit. Although his father was a vagabond and often had severe fights with his son, there was a strange kind of closeness between them.

Two of Smith's immediate family committed suicide. His brother was insanely jealous of his wife, constantly nagging her for no apparent cause. After the poor girl could not endure it any longer, she got away from him the only way she knew how, namely, by taking her own life. When the brother returned home and found her dead, he then killed himself. Also, a sister committed suicide by jumping out of a San Francisco hotel when she was in a drunken stupor. The only relatively normal member of the family was his sister, Barbara, who was now married, but Smith admitted that he often had homicidal feelings toward her.

As to Smith's development, he was arrested for the first time when he was eight. At one time he was placed in an orphanage, and while there, he was severely disciplined for bed wetting. As a young man, he served in the Merchant Marines, and later was in the Army, being stationed in Korea. He received one decoration, but felt he did not receive a deserved promotion because he would not submit to the homosexual needs of a sergeant. He also served a prison sentence in a Kansas penitentiary for breaking and entering. Capote depicts Smith as a very emotionally disturbed person who was able to kill without motive. Being somewhat like a hurt animal, Smith was addicted to aspirin as the result of constant pain resulting from injuries received in a motor cycle accident. So it was Smith, not Hickock, who did the actual killing of the Clutters.

From the brief sketch of the story, we can understand what the crime was and form some impressions about the men who committed it. Now how are we to react to In Cold Blood? First of all, this work affects one emotionally. Usually when one reads a novel, he can become involved with the plot and the characters. If the story itself becomes too threatening, the reader can sit back and say to himself that this is only fiction and escape the unpleasant aspects of the story. But Capote's story will not allow this kind of escape. For the reader has to acknowledge that what the author is reporting has actually happened, if not exactly, at least almost the way he presents it. In other words, rather than being an objective spectator of a crime, the reader becomes a participant emotionally in the crime. So Capote is able to move around our intellectual defenses and to touch us where we really live.

As in the case of The Devils, the problem of evil raises its ugly head again. So we raise the question: how can we account for the way human nature is? What happened to two members of the human species which enabled them in cold blood to murder four other human beings without any provocation whatsoever? What a waste of human life!

Of course, one cannot help but think about the relation of the Clutters to Perry Smith and Richard Hickock. Much of the time Smith was visiting in Alaska with his father, and the Clutters were on their Kansas farm. Should there be a connection between the murderer and the victim? Are the people who are wealthy and powerful responsible for the kind of society that produces people like these criminals? If American society is capable of producing such people as Smith and Hickock, should it be reshaped, or, as Cain responded, when God asked about Abel, "Am I my brother's keeper?"

Either directly or indirectly, Capote raises the question about the responsibility of Smith and Hickock for their actions. As we have already noted, Hickock planned the crime and assisted with it, but Smith did the actual killing. They were tried, found guilty, and punished for their crime. They were treated as if they were mature, rational adults. Whereas Capote thinks they were psychologically sick. If

this were the case, should they have received the death penalty? To raise this question is not to condone what they did,
nor to suggest that such people should be free to run around
in society. There is still another alternative, namely,
to place them in a mental institution for the criminally
insane.

Apart from the literary value of In Cold Blood, which
we have not touched on, this work raises some very profound
moral questions which are not easy to answer and which go
beyond the scope of this study. However, if we place the
story within the context of the Christian story, murder can
only take place after man has been estranged from God.
Once the estrangement has occurred, Cain murdered his brother
Abel. Smith and Hickock were sons of Cain who rose up and
slew their brothers, the Clutters. The Clutters appeared to
be in greater favor with their Creator as evidenced by their
wealth and position in the community, so the modern Cains
were envious of their siblings. Their envy led to robbery
and to the ultimate crime of murder.

2. Paradox

As we continue our examination of the human condition as
revealed in the stories told by dramatists and novelists, we
shall now turn to a work by the Swiss author, Friedrich
Dürrenmatt, entitled, The Physicists.[1] With the possible

---

[1] (New York: Grove Press, 1964), tr. by James Kirkup.

exception of Capote's "non-fiction novel," the works considered thus far have followed a rather traditional style. With Durrenmatt, the style of his two-act play becomes more modernistic, skewing together both the elements of tragedy and comedy.

The story of The Physicists takes place in the drawing room of a large villa, which is set on a hill looking down on a small university town. The villa has been converted into a private mental hospital, patronized by the wealthy of Western Europe. The sanatorium has the popular name of "Les Cerisiers" calling to mind Chekhov's The Cherry Orchard. The time of year is November and the time of day is four in the afternoon.

The founder of the sanatorium is Fraulein Doktor Mathilde Von Zahnd, who is now fifty-five, a hunched back spinster descended from a very prominent family, but acknowledging that she was the only child of a father who hated her. Prior to being converted into a mental hospital, the villa had been the summer home of this well-to-do family. The Fraulein Doktor has the reputation of being a philanthropist and a psychiatrist of enormous repute.

Believing patients with similar interests and backgrounds should be kept together, three insane physicists occupy the drawing room, with their private bedrooms leading off from it. Three months ago one of the physicists murdered his nurse, and now a second nurse has just been murdered by another physicist. The police have arrived, and the inspector is presently attempting to determine the details about the murder in order to make his official report.

The victim was Irene Straub, a twenty-two year old nurse. The murderer is Ernest Heinrich Ernesti, who has the psychotic delusion that he is Albert Einstein. Using the cord of an electric lamp, Ernesti had strangled to death Miss Straub.

The present case is almost a re-enactment of the one that had taken place in August. In the earlier murder, Herbert Georg Beutler, who thinks he is Isaac Newton, strangled his nurse in the same room with the cord from a curtain. In both cases the nurses should have been able to protect themselves, for one was an accomplished woman wrestler and the other was a Judo expert.

A third nurse, Sister Boll, who is a weight lifter, provides the inspector with the necessary information. As the inspector takes the details, she becomes offended when he refers to the murderer as a criminal, for she views him as a sick patient. Also, she refuses to allow the inspector to question him directly, for he is now in his room playing his fiddle with Doktor Zahnd accompanying him on the piano. The inspector is even forced to wait until they have completed their playing before he speaks with the doctor. While he is waiting, the body is carried out.

The physicist, Beutler, who thinks he is Newton, comes

into the drawing room, and the inspector informs him about the murder. Explaining to the inspector that it was his desire to interpret the disorder of nature in an orderly way that led him to become a physicist, Beutler goes about trying to put the disordered room back in order. As the conversation continues, the physicist tells the inspector he is not mad; he killed his nurse because they loved each other, and his "mission is to devote myself to the problems of gravitation, not the physical requirements of a woman."[1] Beutler even confesses he really is not Newton, but Einstein. Since Ernesti is really crazy and thinks he is Einstein, Beutler humors him and allows him to use the name. As the inspector is non-threatening, the physicist tells him that it is the physicists who develop the theories and then the engineers come along and make their machines from the theory. So any fool can come along and turn on a light switch or flip a button and set off the atomic bomb without understanding either. He says he can tell that the inspector does not like him for developing the theory which made the creation of the bomb possible.

When the music stops, the doctor comes into the drawing room to discuss the murder with the inspector. The doctor mentions that although Beutler says in private he is Einstein, he does in fact think he is Newton, for, as the doctor says:

---

[1]Ibid., p. 19.

"It is I who decide who my patients think they are. I know them far better than they know themselves."[1] The inspector informs the doctor about complaints from the prosecutor about the lack of security precautions at the sanitorium, but the doctor assures him there was no way of knowing the patients would strangle their nurses, for their is no medical explanation for their behavior. She suggests that since both physicists were doing research on radio active materials, the dangerous materials may have affected their brains. However, the doctor informs the espector a third physicist lives in this complex. He is Johann Wilhelm Möbius, who has been in the institution for fifteen years. When the inspector insists that male attendants be employed, the doctor agrees to do so. As the inspector departs, the doctor informs Sister Boll that she must hire some male attendants.

Sister Boll tells the doctor that Frau Möbius has arrived and wishes to speak with her. Frau Möbius has divorced her sick husband, and has married Mr. Rose who is going to the Marianas as a missionary. She has with her Möbius' three sons, ages fourteen, fifteen, and sixteen, and she wants them to see their father before they depart for her new husband's assignment.

Frau Rose is five years older than her former husband, Möbius, who is now forty. As a student, Möbius had rented a

---

[1] Ibid., p. 25.

room in the home of his future wife. Frau Rose had helped
him get through high school, and had worked so that he could
study physics at the university. When Möbius was twenty,
they were married, and four years later their first son was
born. When Möbius was on the brink of success in securing
a professorship, he became ill so that he had to be hospitalized. Frau Rose again went to work to pay the increasing
doctors' bills. After fifteen years of loneliness, she
has married Oskar Rose, who brought into the marriage six
sons from his previous marriage. Informing the doctor that
she can no longer pay for Möbius' expenses, the doctor
assures her that she understands and that she can secure
foundation money to keep Möbius in the institution.

When Möbius comes in to visit with his family, they soon
get into a discussion of the sons' vocations. The oldest
desires to become a minister, the middle son wishes to become
a philosopher, and the youngest, who is most like his father,
says that he wants to be a physicist. When Möbius hears the
youngest son's aspirations, he goes into a rage, forbidding
that he pursue it. He says that he would not be in the madhouse today if he had gone into another vocation. Möbius
confesses he is mad, for King Solomon appears to him.
Mr. Rose comes and discusses the plan to go to the South Sea
Islands. The sons then wish to play some music for their
father, but Möbius demands they stop. In fact, he throws a
fit, jumping up on top of a table and repeating "a Song of

Solomon to be sung to the cosmonauts." He movingly says:

> We shagged off into outerspace
> To the deserts of the moon. Foundered in her dust
> Right from the start there were plenty
> That soundlessly shot their bolts out there.
> But most of them cooked
> In the lead fumes of Mercury, were wiped out
> In the oil-swamps of Venus and
> Even on Mars we were wolfed by the sun--
> Thundering, radioactive, yellow.
>
> Jupiter stank
> An arrow-swift rotatory methane mash
> He, the almighty, slung over us
> Till we spewed up our guts over Ganymede....
> Saturn we greeted with curses
> What came next, a waste of breath
>
> Uranus Neptune
> Grayish-green, frozen to death
> Over Pluto and Transpluto fell the final
> Dirty jokes.
> We had long since mistaken the sun for Sirius
> Sirius for Canopus
> Outcasts we cast out, up into the deep
> Toward a few white stars
> That we never reached anyhow
>
> Long since mummied in our spacecraft
> Caked with filth
> In our deathsheads no more memories
> Of breathing earth.[1]

Completing his poem, Möbius demands his family leave, and they

do so feeling their presence has thrown him into a rage.

After the family's departure, Nurse Monika, who has been

Möbius' special nurse, comes to him, and we learn that Möbius'

outburst was spurious, that he had created his fit so the

family would be able to leave him without regrets. The nurse

informs him that she is being transferred to another wing of

---

[1]Ibid., p. 43.

the hospital and that male attendants were being hired to take care of the physicists. Möbius informs Monika that he has been able to accept his lot of being shut up in a madhouse because of her companionship. Monika tells him that she does not think that he is really mad; perhaps, Solomon has revealed to him the secrets of nature, the law about how all things connect, and the Principle of Universal Discovery. She even confesses to Möbius that she loves him, and he in turn acknowledges his love for her.

When Möbius tells Monika that he has not told anyone about the secrets of Solomon, she maintains he should stand up for the revelations. By remaining silent, he may well be betraying the wise king. Also, she tells him she has discussed his case with the doctor and has received her permission for them to be married. In fact, she has taken a position as district nurse outside the hospital, and has taken the liberty to discuss his discoveries with a professor at the university. The professor thinks they might be valid, rather than the works of a madman. When Möbius hears this, he goes into a rage, and reaches for a curtain cord, using it to strangle her to death. With the death of Monika, the first act comes to an end.

The second act takes place in the same drawing room, with the police returning to investigate the third murder. The same inspector Voss, who investigated the other two murders, has returned to take charge of this one. We almost receive the impression that life moves in a cycle with history simply repeating itself. Yet, we begin to sense that something is different, for one thing, the inspector is much calmer. He simply goes about his job, but now the Fräulein Doktor seems very disturbed. She grieves about the death of her "best" nurse, and she even lets slip the phrase "the third murder." Apparently she feels this incident will tarnish her professional reputation, but the inspector is supportive, assuring her she will regain it. To cap it off, when three huge athletic type men come with a food trolley, we know that things have changed.

When the inspector sees them and hears of their backgrounds, he expresses his envy, indicating he would like such men on his police force. The chief attendant is a former European heavy-weight boxing champion. Another attendant is a South American heavyweight boxer, and the third attendant is a black who is the North American middleweight champion. When they set up the food for the three patients, they depart. The doctor informs the inspector the costs for their services is "astronomical."

After the body is removed, Möbius comes into the drawing room, and the doctor reprimands him for killing her best and sweetest nurse. But Möbius explains that King Solomon "ordained" that he do it. Finally, everyone leaves the room with the exception of Möbius and the inspector. Möbius asks the inspector to arrest him, but the inspector says that he could not do that as it was Solomon who ordered it. The inspector explains the three murderers can go unmolested without bothering his conscience. He opines: "For the first time Justice is on holiday--and it's a terrific feeling. Justice, my friend, is a terrible strain; you wear yourself out in its service, both physically and morally."[1]

When the inspector departs, Beutler comes into the drawing room. He tells Möbius they now have male attendants. He also confesses to Möbius that he is not really mad and wants to leave the madhouse. His real identity is not Newton, nor even Beutler, but it is Alec Jaspar Kilton, a famous physicist who came to the hospital to learn about Möbius. When his nurse began to suspect that he was not mad, he murdered her in order to prove his insanity. Kilton informs Möbius that he and the Intelligence Service he represents consider him the greatest physicist of all times. Upon reading one of Möbius' published works, it finally dawned on him the author was a genius. So the Intelligence Service trained him in order that he might come to the hospital.

In the background is Ernesti who has overheard the conversation. He comes in and tells them he is not mad, nor Einstein, but he is Joseph Eisler, another famous physicist, who is working in the Intelligence Service of his country. Eisler also acknowledges he killed his nurse because she was

---

[1]Ibid., p. 65.

becoming suspicious that he was not mad. Realizing that none of the physicists are mad, they sit down to enjoy their meal. However, their relaxation is short lived. The three attendants return, letting down some metal grilles over the windows giving the hospital the appearance of a prison. Although the two physicists from the Intelligence Service want to escape, Möbius indicates he has no desire for escape. As they discuss their situation, Möbius acknowledges he has solved the problem of gravitation, discovered the Unitary Theory of Elementary Particles, and even solved the Principle of Universal Discovery. He explains that if his discoveries were to be made known, the results could be devastating to the human race. He has destroyed his manuscripts, and he pleads with the other physicists to remain with him in the madhouse in order to protect the world. Möbius points out that he killed his nurse in order to avoid a great disaster, and they must be able to sacrifice themselves for all minkind.

Although the two physicists give their counter arguments, Möbius is finally able to persuade them to stay with him. He believes it is the most rational and moral thing for them to do. Although they regret the necessity of having to do so, they soothe their consciences about killing the nurses by maintaining they did the killings for a higher cause. So each man returns to his room committed to the belief he should remain in the madhouse.

The next time the attendants appear they come dressed in

black official uniforms, with pistols at their sides. The
Fräulein Doktor returns and places a portrait of her father,
who was an army general, on the wall. She then sends for the
physicists. When they arrive, she informs them she has overheard their conversations and knows their true identitites.
She asks the attendants to take the intelligence men's guns
and radio transmitters, and to leave her alone with the
physicists. She confesses to them that King Solomon appears
to her, indicating she is really insane. She criticizes
Möbius for keeping secret what Solomon had revealed to him,
believing he was betraying the king by doing so. She says:
"But Möbius betrayed him. He tried to keep secret what could
not be kept secret. For what was revealed to him was no secret.
Because it could be thought. Everything that can be thought
is thought at some time or another. Now or in the future.
What Solomon had found could be found by anyone, but he wanted
it to belong to himself alone, his means toward the establish-
ment of his holy dominion over all the world. And so he did
seek me out, his unworthy handmaiden."[1]

The insane Fräulein Doktor explains that Solomon has
instructed her to cast Möbius down and reign in his place.
Over the years she has administered to Möbius drugs, which
enabled her to take his secrets from him and she has photo-
copies of them. She has used his discoveries to gain large

---

[1]Ibid., p. 89.

sums of money. With the organization of her cartel, she ultimately intends to control the world. When Möbius hears this, he tells her that he was just faking, but she maintains he is just lying. She goes on to explain how she manipulated the three physicists so they would murder their nurses. The murders allowed her to keep the men incarcerated.

When the doctor finally departs, Möbius realizes that she at least spoke one truth, namely, what was once thought can never be unthought. The physicists now realize the world has fallen into the hands of an insane female psychiatrist. With their plan foiled and their escape impossible, each physicist marches to the center of the stage and announces his name as a madman and offers a brief comment about his assumed identity. First Kilton says he is Newton and returns to his room; next Eisler announces he is Einstein and goes, and finally Möbius says he is poor King Solomon. The story comes to an end with all the characters off stage and the fiddle playing in the background.

As we step back to look at the play, we can see that act one appears to be a straightforward presentation of a story in which three ordinary murders take place inside an exclusive, private, mental hospital. All three murders are committed by three madmen, who are in their professions, physicists. The hospital is run by a world famous female psychiatrist, who is noted for both her medical skill and her philanthropic activity. The world is rational and well ordered, for we know, for certain, who is crazy and who is sane. Hence, we are able to make sense of the action, finding it almost comic, or so we think.

Act two does a complete flip-flop. What we thought was the truth on closer inspection turns out to be error. Things are completely reversed. The three physicists, whom we thought were mad, are actually sane, and the female psychiatrist, whom we thought was sane and altruistic, turns out to be nuttier than a fruitcake with a megalomaniac desire to control the world. The levity of the first act takes on a deadly seriousness in the second act. The mood quickly changes from the comic to the tragic.

The kind of paradoxical tension, which exists between the two acts, permeates the whole drama. Just at the moment Möbius and Monika proclaim their love for each other and are on the brink of leaving the sanitarium, stepping out to their freedom, Möbius murders the woman he loves and seals the entrance to freedom. So Dürrenmatt raises an issue about man's ability to rationally plan his destiny. The most rational schemes go awry.

Closely associated with this problem is the problem of the relationship of morality to science. The scientist is not simply a well precisioned machine; he is a human being, and, as such, he has to make value judgments. How ought he to relate his morality to the work he is doing? Does he have any moral responsibility for his discoveries which are potentially harmful to the human race. Dürrenmatt, it seems to me, provides a careful analysis to this problem.

First, in the character of Kilton (Beutler), who apparently represents a Western power such as the United States,
the position is taken that science is an autonomous discipline.
The scientist must be free to do his research, and what he is
doing is done in a moral vacuum. He has no moral responsibility for what his country or its military do with his
discoveries. For his dedication to science, the outstanding
one will be given public honors such as the Nobel Prize.
He also will be paid generously, and will be provided excellent working facilities.

On the other hand, Eisler, a representative physicist
from an Eastern country such as the Soviet Union, offers a
second alternative. He does not think the scientist should
work in a moral and political vacuum, but rather he should
commit himself to some ideology such as Marxism and work
through some party such as the communist. Once he has committed himself he will use his discoveries to promote his
ideology and party. He too will be adequately cared for and
receive recognition for serving the party.

Möbius, of course, represents a third alternative. He
thinks the scientist must be rational in making his decisions,
and he argues whether one goes with the capitalist or the
communist, he is forfeiting his freedom. In neither situation
does the scientist have any control over how his discoveries
will be used. Thus, Möbius maintains the scientist cannot

separate his work from his moral responsibility. He is
responsible for his research and how it will be used. With
this the case, he says his own discoveries are potentially
destructive to the human race. He believes his knowledge is
so dangerous that it must be suppressed; so he has feigned
madness, even murdered his nurse in the name of a higher good,
the survival of mankind. Both Kilton and Eisler are persuaded by Möbius' logic and agree to remain in the madhouse
as madmen in order to save humanity.

But in Dürrenmatt's topsy-turvy world Möbius' answer
is not sufficient. For one thing, what can once be thought
can be thought again. It is just a matter of time until
some young genius comes along and makes the same discovery
that Möbius made. Also, the insane, evil female psychiatrist
had Möbius' room bugged, stealing his manuscripts by making
xeroxed copies of them. Using these discoveries, she has
established a large cartel and in time intends to control
the world by blackmailing it. In a sense, she represents
a kind of fourth alternative, namely exploiting science for
one's personal gain.

None of these four alternatives appear to be adequate.
Möbius is obviously correct in wanting to bring to bear the
moral dimension in dealing with science, but he is wrong in
thinking that knowledge can be suppressed or hidden indefinite-
ly. So implicit, not explicit, within the drama is the
conviction that what concerns all must be decided by all

for every man has a vested interest in the consequences.

Although Dürrenmatt is the son of a Protestant minister and has been greatly influenced by the works of such influential thinkers as Soren Kierkegaard, he obviously does not believe the religious institution, as it is currently operating, has much to offer in dealing with such an important and complicated problem. Oskar Rose, the missionary, goes off to the peaceful Mariana islands rather than remaining where the action is and offering moral guidance. However, there is no doubt that Möbius stands within the tradition of Jesus, for he is willing to sacrifice himself for the good of humanity. Although we may question his reasoning and even his sacrifice of Nurse Monika, we cannot help but respect him and his moral commitment. Obviously Dürrenmatt's exposure to the Christian story has had an influence on his own vision and sensitivity, but there is no clear indication that Möbius should be viewed as a committed Christian. His motivation appears to be more a humanistic concern for his fellowman than one based on some kind of commitment to man's Creator. One writer has said: "From the beginning of his career, Dürrenmatt has been deeply concerned with moral and religious values. His strict Protestant training and his early interest in Kierkegaard and Kafka may help explain his preoccupation with sin, suffering and the quest for redemption in a seemingly alien or indifferent universe."

3. Silence

One of the stories, taken over from Judaism by Christianity, is the story about the ancient Hebrews migrating into Egypt and being allowed to settle in the land of Goshen. With the passing of time, the Hebrews increased in numbers and were prosperous. As they increased, the pharoah became afraid of them. In order to deal with this fear, he passed a decree making the Hebrews slaves. He used the slaves to carry out his ambitious building projects. But the Hebrews continued to multiply and posed an imagined threat to the pharoah. Thus, he passed another decree, stating that all Hebrew male infants must be drowned at birth. By killing off the males, he knew that he could cut down on their number and thus their threat.

Although this story came to a head in the thirteenth century before the present era with the birth of Moses, the story was prophetic of what was to be the Jewish experience throughout history. In Germany and many countries in Europe in the nineteen-thirties, fear and envy of the Jews were rampant and were expressed in the vilest anti-Semitism. There arose a new pharoah in the person of Adolf Hitler, who was committed to finding a solution to the "Jewish problem." Like his ancient Egyptian counterpart, he treated them like slaves; and following the example of Cain, he shipped them off to death camps especially designed for them. But his solution went way beyond that of destroying the male infants, for he

desired to liquidate all Jews: men, women, old, and young
alike.

The horrors of Hitler's genocide program have been
indelibly etched in the psyche of all Jews. Perhaps no
Jewish story teller is more persuasive in relating this tragic
tale than Elie Wiesel in such works as Night and Gates of the
Forest. However, Christians have not only made the ancient
story their story, but they have been profoundly affected by
this modern tragedy. No dramatist, it seems to me, has raised
the implications of this story for Christians more forcefully
than Rolf Hochhuth in his controversial drama, The Deputy.[1]
This play opened in West Berlin on February 20, 1963. No
drama of this period caused so much excitement. As it appeared
in several cities throughout Europe, some people defended it,
whereas others attacked it. Following its premiere in the
United States on February 26, 1964, Americans also reacted
strongly to the play, with some thinking the message was
valid and with others feeling the play should be muffled.

What is the play all about? What makes it cause so much
excitement? The Deputy is a long play, containing five acts
broken down into eleven scenes. If the whole play were produced, it would last from six to eight hours. The setting is
Europe, mostly Germany and a little Rome, during the war
years of 1942-43. The play deals with people who were involved

---

[1](New York: Grove Press, 1964), tr. by Richard and
Clara Winston.

directly or indirectly with the mass murder of the European Jews by the Nazis. In this story, Hochhuth attempts to recapture the blackest period in human history, for approximately six million Jews were gassed and cremated, not because of their involvement in the war effort, but because they happened to be Jews. Bigotry and anti-Semitism reached their tragic peaks during these years.

Although the scenes are varied, they depict dramatically various aspects of this historical tragedy. In a sense the scenes blend into a drab mosaic, creating a mood of shock and horror for the audience. Some of the scenes take place inside various ecclesiastical offices of the Roman Catholic Church, for the play moves from the Nuncio's office in Berlin to the Papal Palace in the Vatican. Another scene takes place in the apartment of a Nazi officer, who was protectively concealing a Jewish man; we sense the tension and anxiety of the officer because of his fear of being discovered. One of the most moving scenes shows a Jewish family taken from their Roman apartment by the Nazis, almost under the window of the Pope. Still other scenes transpire at Auschwitz, where it has been estimated that over three-and-one-half-million Jews were gassed. Through the various dialogues, the author enables the audience to sense something of the despair and inhumanity experienced by the victims.

The plot of the story is not difficult to follow. Most of the action centers around two people. The first is a

young Jesuit, Father Riccardo Fontana, whose own father is
a lay economic advisor to the Vatican. The second is Kurt
Gerstein, who is a professing Christian and who has joined
the SS to obtain proof of the genocide program, hoping to
save as many lives as possible. The action begins when
Gerstein forces his way into the Nuncio's office in Berlin,
informing the Nuncio in the presence of the newly arrived
Father Fontana that as many as ten thousand Jews were being
murdered a day. Gerstein then insists that the church, through
the Pope, must speak out against this destruction of European
Jewry. As a result of this meeting, Father Fontana becomes
actively concerned about the tragic fate of those who wear
"the Star of David." Ultimately he ends up in Rome, pleading
with the "Vicar of Christ" himself to protest against those
who are imposing the incomprehensible cruelty on the Jewish
people. However, Fontana is unable to persuade Pope Pius
XII to break his silence. Feeling the futility of the situation, the young priest concludes that it is his Christian
obligation to go to Auschwitz and suffer with the condemned.
So the play ends with the priest being shot to death in the
presence of Gerstein, whose Jewish sympathies have been exposed, and Jacobson, a Jew, who had been unsuccessfully
befriended by both Fontana and Gerstein. As the priest dies,
the Nazi doctor, representing the embodiment of evil, cynically
refuses to aid the cleric.   ·

The Deputy is a powerful play, for it attempts to remind

us of a very black period in the history of civilized man.
We are reminded that churchmen and Christians gave their
support to the Nazi mania. Educated men, cultured men,
sophisticated businessmen, men with scientific and medical
skill too easily jumped on the Nazi bandwagon. Often scientists would gas Jews in the daytime, put on their tails in the
evening, and enjoy with their wives the culture provided by
Germany's large cities. Only a handful out of the millions
of Germans had the convictions and the courage to condemn
the sadistic, cruel behavior of the Nazis. Today, we are
still stunned when we think about Hitler's Germany. Why
was it able to happen? Could it happen again?

In this work, Hochhuth does not embrace a pacifist
position. He assumes that war brings destruction and suffering to both sides; so his play is not a protest against
war as such. However, he places the cruelty suffered by the
Jews in a category by itself. The Jews were chosen by Hitler
to be exterminated; this was the most extreme form of anti-
Semitism. Hitler wanted to destroy the Jews, many of whom
were native Germans. His treatment of the Jews need have
little to do with his war effort. It was possible, then,
for a German to condone Hitler's war, and at the same time to
bitterly denounce his anti-Semitism. It also would follow
that a churchman, who wanted to remain "neutral" throughout
the war, could also protest against the genocide program.
War is one thing; killing men and women by the millions

simply because they happen to be a member of a certain minority group is something altogether different.

The most controversial part of the play, at least for the Roman Catholic, is act four. The setting is the Papal Palace and Father Fontana and Pius XII are discussing the position of the church with respect to the Jewish massacre. During the conversation, the Pope makes the following points in justifying his position. (1) He is doing all in his power to help the Jews. Many are being hidden away in monasteries and protected by priests. (2) He is in sympathy with those who speak in behalf of the persecuted. (3) He must be judicious, for Hitler could bring his hostility to bear more directly against the Roman Catholic Church in Germany. The property of the church and investments could be confiscated. (4) The Pope also views his role as mediator, for he may well be the one to mediate between Hitler and the Allies when the war is finally concluded. He, therefore, must maintain his neutrality. (5) The Pope sees clearly the threat of Russia and the possibility of communism's takeover of Western Europe. In other words, Hitler is fulfilling an important political function, serving as a buffer between Western Europe and Russia. This is based on a strong and lasting fear the Church has had of communism. (6) Finally, the Pope is willing to make a general statement condemning man's inhumanity to man, but he is unwilling to condemn clearly and specifically Hitler's acts of violence against the Jews.

It is the opinion of Father Fontana that in extreme times the Church must take an extreme position. Pope Pius XII, as the religious head of five-hundred-million people, including twenty percent of the German people, ought to protest strongly against the Nazi treatment of the Jews. The priest thinks it will have a positive effect on Hitler, and, too, there are times when the Church must take a stand, regardless of the consequences because a particular position is right. The first Vicar of Christ experienced martyrdom, and it might be that the present Vicar must also risk being martyred. The priest, to say the least, is disappointed with the Pope. In his presence, he attaches the Star of David to his coat, walking out determined to go to Auschwitz to suffer with the Jews.

It seems to me that act four should not lead one to conclude that Hochhuth is a narrow-minded Protestant who is trying to pass the responsibility for the Jewish massacres on to the shoulders of Pope Pius XII. To draw this inference is to be less than fair to Hochhuth. He places the responsibility for the "Jewish solution" firmly in the lap of the German people. He also acknowledges those Roman Catholic priests who died because of their protests against the Nazi extermination program. Father Fontana, one of the central characters in the story, loses his life for the Jews. In interviews, Hochhuth has even praised Pius XI because of his criticism of the anti-Semites.

The author's real concern is with the silence of Pius
II. His criticism is not focused on the entire Roman
atholic Church, nor on all the popes. His criticism is leveled
gainst the actions or inactions of Pope Pius XII. In effect,
ochhuth is saying that the greater the ability and the
esponsibility a person has the more we expect from that
erson. We do not judge the village idiot by the same stan-
ards as the President of the United States. Likewise we do
ot expect as much of a parish priest in a small isolated
illage as we do of the Pope. When a man is honored with the
ighest office in Christendom, we are disappointed when his
erformance does not measure up to the position he has ac-
epted. It obviously is the opinion of Hochhuth that Pope
ius XII did not act as the Roman Pontiff should have during
he massacre of the Jews. Pius XII was perhaps one of the
ost intelligent and well-informed men of his generation.
e could have spoken clearly and decisively against the death
amps, but he chose to remain silent. If a man with less
bility and in a position with less respect had remained
ilent, it may not be as disturbing. In a sense, the extra-
rdinary intelligence and ability of Pius XII tends to condemn
im. Although Pius XII claimed to be the "Vicar of Christ
n earth" and although he had the highest ecclesiastical office
n earth, his decision on the Jewish q uestion was not great.
t was extremely medoicre.

It, however, is not too difficult to see why some Roman

Catholics might think The Deputy is an anti-Catholic play.
At the time it appeared, many Catholics did not understand
the "Protestant mind." Protestants do not believe that any
man or any institution is infallible. Infallibility is a
characteristic that can apply only to God. However, the
Roman Catholic believes that the Pope is infallible when he
speaks ex cathedra, on the subjects of faith and morals, and
speaks for the universal church. When he speaks on other
subjects, the Roman Catholic wants to lend a respectful
ear. Thus, when a man, especially a non-Catholic, critically
questions some action of a Roman Pontiff, he, to many Roman
Catholics, is questioning the doctrine of Papal infallibility.
Naturally the Roman Catholic feels obligated to defend the
person who plays such an important part in his religion.
In part, this accounts, it seems to me, for the strong emotional protests against The Deputy.

We can react to this play in a variety of ways. We
can view it as a modern drama, for this is what it is. We
can argue about whether or not it is a good play. What about
the plot? Are the characters believable and real? Now these
are important questions, and they have a place, but I would
hope that we might feel obligated to move beyond the level
of the drama critic. Also, we can become preoccupied with the
historical accuracy of the drama. Obviously the historical
facts are important, but we must not become so involved with
the historical details that we pass the play off as raising

no moral questions. Likewise, we can become involved with the abstract problem of ethics. The ethical question involving the silence of Pope Pius XII toward the slaughter of European Jewry is most important, and Hochhuth wants to raise it. There is a place for discussing and evaluating it. However, I would think that we might move beyond the "academic" considerations of the story to the existential and religious considerations.

In one scene, Hochhuth raises a very personal question about God. Why did God remain silent while millions of his people were being gassed to death? The satanic doctor looked at Auschwitz as a kind of testing of God, for he says to Father Fontana:

> First you can watch me for a year or so
> conducting this, the boldest experiment
> that man has ever undertaken...
> I took the vow to challenge the Old Gent,
> to provoke him so limitlessly
> that he would have to give an answer.
> Even if only the negative answer
> which can be his sole excuse, as
> Stendhal put it: that He doesn't exist...
> Well, hear the answer: not a peep
> came from heaven, not a peep
> for fifteen months,
> Not once since I've been giving tourists
> tickets to Paradise.[1]

But this play not only raises the question about the silence of God; it also raises the question about the silence of man. It is not too difficult to draw the inference that Hochhuth is maintaining that man is responsible for his behavior.

---

[1]*Ibid.*, p. 247.

He is likewise responsible for his actions. A man's actions should be responsible and good, but this is not all that he is saying. He is not going to let us off the hook this easily. For he contends that man is responsible for his refusing to act. In other words, man is held accountable for his silence. To remain silent in the midst of evil is to enhance the evil.

In order that we not escape this important point of Hochhuth, let me bring it right to our own door. If a man lives in a community where racial discrimination is practiced, and if he remains silent, even though he does not perform the acts of discrimination himself, he is guilty, for his silence enables the discrimination to continue. If a man works for a company where illegal "price fixing" is practiced, and if he knows about it, but does not speak out against it, he is guilty, for his silence permits the price fixing to continue. If a man is a member of a political party, where immoral "dirty tricks" are practiced, and if he knows it, but does not speak out against it, he is guilty, for his silence allows the illegal, undemocratic practice to continue. We, therefore, do not have to discriminate, nor do the price fixing, nor engage in the dirty tricks ourselves, but to the degree that we allow these practices to exist without registering our disapproval, we are guilty. Pope Pius XII most surely did not perform acts of violence against the Jews, but Hochhuth is saying that his silence to some extent condemns him.

Before leaving The Deputy, we should raise the question about our own consciences. We ought to try to determine whether or not we have any anti-Semitism in ourselves, or whether we possess any prejudice against any member of God's creation. All anti-Semitism did not vanish with the death of Hitler, neither did all anti-Catholicism, nor anti-Negroidism, nor, for what it is worth, anti-Protestantism. Our communities are still infected with these prejudices. The Nazi "solution" was the result of the logic of these same prejudices being carried to its bizarre conclusion.

Setting aside the dramatic weaknesses of The Deputy, Hochhuth has done us a service. He has forced us to look back on a tragic historical story that needs critical evaluation, but he has done more, for he has forced us to look at ourselves. He has reminded us that we do not have to commit unjust acts ourselves to be guilty. We are guilty when we remain silent and do not protest against the injustices imposed on others. Also, as in the case of Whiting and Capote, he has reminded us that we, too, have the capacity to do acts of evil. By forcing us to recognize this aspect of our nature, Hochhuth has made us take a step in the right direction. For the first step in learning to deal with a problem is to learn that there is a problem.

4. Conclusion

As the Christian interprets the human condition, he
views man as originally being created by God and being in
harmony with Him and the universe. But then man rebelled
against his Creator and alienated himself from the Source of
authentic existence. In this state of alienation, man is
destined to live, and the way he now lives is inauthentic.
The human condition in its inauthentic form has been characterized in Romans by sin, suffering, and death. In the past
two chapters, we have examined six stories as told by literary
artists. We have interpreted these modern stories from the
perspective of man's alienation. So man, as a sinner, feels
an emptiness, creates evil, engages in self-deception, commits murder, confronts paradox, and remains silent. The vision
of man presented by these modern writers is neither pleasant
nor encouraging, but neither is the vision of man as depicted
in the Christian story.

Perhaps Robert Penn Warren in All The King's Men best
summarizes the conclusion reached by both the modern teller
of stories and the Christian story. Representing the Southern
politician or more specifically Huey Long, Boss goes to a
well-known physician to persuade him to become the head of a
hospital soon to be built. The doctor has remained honest by
withdrawal into the simple decisions of his uneventful life
and profession. His tranquility is disturbed because Boss
wants him to become the director of a great hospital that has

come about as the result of brass egotism and political manipulations.   In spite of the questionable circumstances which
have paved the way for the hospital to come into existence,
the hospital can be used for doing good.   Boss explains:

"Goodness, Yeah, just plain simple goodness. Well you
can't inherit that from anybody. You got to make it,
Doc. If you want it. And you got to make it out of
badness. Badness. And you know why, Doc?" He raised
his bulk up in the broken-down wretch of an overstuffed
chair he was in, and leaned forward, his hands on his
knees, his elbows cocked out, his head outthrust and the
hair coming down in his eyes, and stared into Adam's
face. "Out of badness," he repeated. "And you know
why? Because there isn't anything else to make it out of."
Then, sinking into the wreck, he asked softly, "Did you
know that, Doc?" Adam didn't say a word. Then the
Boss asked, softer still, almost whispering, "Did you
know that, Doc?"[1]

[1](New York: Bantam Books, 1959), p. 257.

CHAPTER V

SUFFERING

No religious problem is more difficult for the Christian
than the problem of suffering. The problem arises from the
fact that the Christian maintains that God is both all-
powerful and all-loving and yet suffering exists. If suffering were a delusion and hence not real, all that would
need to be done is to overcome the delusion. Or if we
maintain that God is limited in power, there would be no
problem. For suffering would then be explicable on the grounds
of God's lack of power to overcome it. Or if we said that
God is not all-loving, the problem would be solved. For if
evil existed in God, he might wish to express it to man in
the form of suffering.

In our consideration of sin, we have skirted around the
problem of suffering. We have seen it in both interpersonal
relationships and in the social sphere. In The Devils we
saw how institutions are permeated with evil and how eventually the Priest Grandier was made to suffer because of it.
We came upon it in In Cold Blood in the senseless murders of
the Clutters, and we encountered it again in The Deputy in
the Nazi genocide program against the Jews.

Two modern works, which have pushed the problem of

suffering to center stage, are Archibald MacLeish's <u>J. B.</u> and Albert Camus' <u>The Plague</u>. Although neither of these works will offer a completely adequate solution for the Christian, they will throw some important light on the subject. Hence, we shall look at these two stories about human woe.

1. <u>"Blow on the coal of the heart."</u>

MacLeish tells his story about <u>J. B.</u> in a drama with eleven scenes, preceded by a prologue.[1] The story itself takes place inside a circus tent, off in the area where the side-show is held. The crowd has gone home, leaving the tent empty with the exception of two circus vendors: Mr. Zuss and Nickles. The vendors are two broken down actors who have fallen on hard times. They begin to discuss the ancient story of Job in the Bible, and, before long, they raise the question as to whether they should act it out. They decide to do so. Zuss will play God, and Nickles will play Satan. Although Nickles thought he should play Job, Zuss convinces him that almost any poor wretched human being in any country of the world and in any period in history can play that part. Heaven is located on a platform, somewhat like a crow's nest overlooking the stage which is earth, the locale for the re-enactment of the story. So each of the broken down actors takes his mask and begins to speak his parts. As the lights dim, the illumination focuses on the stage where J. B., the modern Job, appears with his family.

---

[1](Boston: Houghton Mifflin Co., 1956).

The parents are sitting at an affluent, sumptuous table
with their five beautiful children, ranging in ages from
six through thirteen. They are well attended by two buxom,
middle-aged maids. J. B. offers his thanksgiving blessing,
and as he serves the turkey, Sarah, his wife, becomes very
serious, trying to get the family to reflect carefully on
the importance of this day and their many blessings. J. B.
assures her that God has been on his side as evidenced by his
prosperity. However, Sarah feels that her husband has been
blessed because he deserves it. She argues that God is just,
and if J. B. did not deserve his prosperity, then God would
not have given it to him.

Following the scene at the dinner table, the focus
returns to Zuss and Nickles. (Moving the focus from the
stage to the crow's nest and back again is generally followed
throughout the play.) Zuss opines that J. B. will make an
excellent Job, for "he has the wealth, the wife, the children,
Position in the world."[1] He loves God and is a "perfect and
upright man." Nickles indicates that he does not like him,
but he argues that if all these good things are taken from
him, he will sing a different tune. However, Zuss disagrees
with his antagonist, for he believes nothing will be able to
destroy J. B.'s faith in and praise of God. The conflict is
established, and now we must see which man is correct in his

[1]Ibid., p. 45.

assessment. The two actors place their masks on again, letting the audience know that J. B. will lose everything, but his life.

The stage lights return to the home of J. B. Obviously several years have passed, for the oldest son, David, is now away in the army. Two drunken soldiers come to the home, seeking a handout, but their plans go askew when they learn that J. B. has not been informed about the death of his son. The son had died after the truce had been announced because of an officer's stupidity. After they break the tragic news to the family, we realize that the time for J. B.'s testing has come in earnest.

Before long a second message arrives. This time the bad news is brought by newspapermen. They inform J. B. and Sarah that their two children have been out riding with a youth who was drinking. There had been a severe automobile accident at a high rate of speed, and four people were killed. Two of the dead were their children, Mary and Jonathan. As the parents discuss the mishap, Sarah reminds her husband when things were going well for them, he attributed their good fortune to God, but now that misfortune had come their way, he attributed it to chance.

When it rains, it pours misfortune for J. B. This time two police officers come, seeking information about their youngest daughter, Rebecca. In the process of the inquiry, it becomes obvious that a young girl has been raped and killed

by an idiot out behind the lumber yard. The victim of this
cruel crime is their daughter, who was most like her father.
Upon receiving this cruel news, J. B. responds: "the Lord
giveth...Lord taketh away!"

The next catastrophe to hit this family is an explosion,
which destroys J. B.'s bank and plant causing him to lose
millions. Sarah was present when the explosion occurred.
Two workers found her under the debris and took her home,
where they explain to J. B. what has happened. And Sarah
informs him they have lost their final child, Ruth, in the
accident. Trying to comfort her, J. B. assures his wife that
God is present in their desperation, and so he affirms once
again the ancient words of Job: "The Lord giveth ... the
Lord taketh away ... Blessed be the name of the Lord."[1]

After all these mishaps, the play returns to Zuss and
Nickles. Nickles confesses that he is utterly provoked with
J. B. for enduring his hardships and still praising God.
However, Zuss feels that J. B.'s response is simply wonderful.
He is still able to say "yea" to life and to the world; he
utters his affirmation in the midst of his unfathomable
suffering. As Nickles is not satisfied, he suggests they
carry the game of life one step further, allowing suffering
to touch the body of J. B. He believes that J. B. will then
either commit suicide, i.e., "reject the whole creation

---

[1]Ibid., pp. 89-90.

with a stale pink pill," or else "spit" at the creation.
As to be expected, Zuss does not share his prognosis, for he
is certain J. B. will endure till the very end and "his
suffering will praise God." So J. B.'s hardships are not
over, for he must continue until one or the other of the cos
mic players concedes defeat.

Waiting for the sufferings of J. B. to resume, they hear
a distant voice speak the lines of God. Nickles explains that
it must have been the prompter reading the lines, wishing fo
them to continue with the story. So they replace their
masks, as we look down at J. B. who is now in rags and whose
body is covered with sores. Sarah is by his side. Several
women pass, knowing who the sufferers are and explaining their
misfortunes. In the depths of agony J. B. calls out to God
to let him die, but Sarah cynically points out that God will
not even assist him with that. She now feels that God is
their enemy; however, J. B. maintains that God still has
something hidden from them which he will later reveal. As
he tries to understand his situation, he feels that he must
be guilty of some sin to deserve such punishment, for he knows
that God is just. Sarah disagrees, and in referring to the
deaths of her children, she says she will not sacrifice their
deaths "to make injustice justice and God good!"[1] Not being
able to endure their situation any longer, Sarah leaves her

---

[1]Ibid., p. 110.

husband, who cries out to God to show him his guilt.

While alone on the rubbish heap, J. B. is visited by three comforters. One is Bildad, representing Marxism. A second is Eliphaz, representing psychiatry, and a third is Zophar, representing the modern minister. Of the three, only the minister believes that guilt is legitimate and real. So J. B. asks him to show him his sin in order that he might know why it is that he suffers. However, Zophar explains that the sin does not have to be named to know that one needs forgiveness. What J. B. needs above all else is to "repent." Drawing upon a rather sterile view of original sin, he explains that J. B.'s sin is that he was born a man. But J. B. insists he will not confess his sin until he knows what it is. He will not violate his integrity.

A voice out of the distance speaks to the sufferer, overwhelming him with questions such as "where wast thou when I laid the foundation of the earth..." Upon hearing this strange voice, the comforters decide to depart. The voice continues its questioning of J. B. until finally he repents for having questioned the Almighty and trying to get him to justify his human suffering.

With J. B. prostrated before the voice of the Almighty, the focus returns to Zuss and Nickles. At long last Nickles admits that Zuss got the better of him, for he acknowledges that Zuss was magnificent. J. B. did not curse God; instead, he bowed down and repented. Nevertheless, Nickles notes that

the outcome does not necessarily mean that Zuss is right.
Zuss then reminds him the story is not yet over. J. B. will
have everything restored to him, i.e., wealth, wife, and
even other children. Yet, Nickles doubts that after what
J. B. has been through, he will be able to pick up the pieces
and begin all over again. As the two conclude their discussion, they return to their vendor's aprons with their balloons
and popcorn. As Nickles looks down in the ring, he sees
J. B. and goes to him, telling him how the story will end,
namely everything will be restored even his health.

The final scene shows Sarah returning to her husband
with a twig of forsythia in her hand. She explains how she
found it growing in the debris and ashes. As they reflect
on their awful experience, she explains there is no justice,
only the world. She confesses that it was because she loved
him that she went away as she could not help him any more.
As they begin the task of straightening things up, she says
to J. B.:

> Blow on the coal of the heart.
> The candles in churches are out.
> The lights have gone out in the sky.
> Blow on the coal of the heart
> And we'll see by and by...[1]

And he responds: "we'll know" as the play ends.

MacLeish with creative imagination has powerfully retold
the ancient story of Job. And in his retelling, he contends

---

[1] Ibid., p. 153.

there is no apparent relationship between sin and suffering.
J. B. was truly an upright man, and yet he suffered. Hence,
the good and righteous man might well suffer. Simply because
one is good, this does not necessarily mean he will not suffer.
And a further inference is that although one might prosper,
this does not mean that he is not evil.

As we have seen, the modern comforters offered their
solutions to J. B. The Marxist contends that J. B.'s attempt
to establish a connection between his suffering and his guilt
is fruitless. In fact, he should not even feel guilty.
Guilt is simply a hold over from an earlier bygone era. As
history runs inexorably along its economically determined
course, individuals will suffer. But the suffering of the
individual is not important, for ultimately suffering will be
brought to an end. In the future both guilt and suffering
will vanish from history. As for the psychiatrist, he
suggests that the victim's difficulty springs from the Oedi-
pus Complex. In other words, as a youth, J. B. wished to
displace his father and take his place in the affections of
his mother. Although he has repressed this childhood fantasy,
it comes back to haunt him in the form of guilt which he does
not understand. By recognizing the genesis of his problem,
he should now be able to solve it. Of course, the cleric
maintains the guilt is real. To be born a man is to feel
guilty. There is no other explanation for it, so J. B. ought
to confess his guilt and repent. The cleric is obviously

trying to exploit his guilt. When the comforters depart,
J. B. is no better than when they arrived. It is when the
voice of God comes to him out of the distant whirlwind and
overwhelms him that he is able to accept his human condition.
Although he bows to the divine majesty, this really does
not solve his problem.

Although MacLeish follows faithfully the biblical story
of Job which ends on an affirmation of faith in the Creator,
when the mysterious voice of God breaks through, his own
position appears closer to that of Sarah, which is much
more skeptical. His answer seems to be that the universe is
indifferent to man. There is no justice, i.e., a correlation
between a man's sin and his suffering. Yet, in the midst of
this indifferent and uncaring universe, where man experiences
both different kinds and various degrees of suffering, there
is the continuation of life as exemplified in the blooming of
the forsythia, and there is a glow of love in the human heart
as seen in Sarah at the end. If the coal is carefully blown
on, it might burst into a warm flame.

Unless I misunderstand MacLeish, his position is not
characteristically Christian. His position is more that of a
positive humanist. It is a position which the Christian can
appreciate, but he must go beyond it. For the Christian,
although the universe at times may appear indifferent, it is
in fact, friendly. This friendliness may be revealed in
human life, but, if for some reason unknown to man it is not,

it will be revealed in the life to come.

2. "Outraged By The Whole Scheme Of Things."

As is MacLeish, Albert Camus also is concerned with the problem of suffering. His work, which deals specifically with this problem, is The Plague,[1] which many consider to be his greatest literary work. Two extreme attitudes toward suffering are seen in the characters of a priest and a doctor. Hence we shall focus basically on them as we examine this important work.

The story takes place in one of the years of the 1940's at Oran, which is a seacoast town in Algiers. It is a hot, dry, ugly city of about two-hundred thousand inhabitants. Dr. Bernard Rieux is the narrator of the story although he does not reveal his identity until the very end. His reporting is rather detached and objective, i.e., the kind of reporting one might expect from a man carefully trained in the sciences. The action begins in mid-April when a few dead rats are discovered in various parts of the city. The number of dead rats increases each day until on a single day eight thousand are collected to be burned. Following the incineration of the rats, people begin to come down with a sickness. At first a few die and the number increases until there is an epidemic. In time the disease is diagnosed as bubonic plague. Because of the seriousness of the epidemic, the administration is

---

[1](New York: The Modern Library, 1948), tr. by Stuart Gilbert.

forced to close off the city, refusing to allow anyone to leave for fear they will spread the disease. As the plague passes along its destructive course, it reaches such gigantic proportions that schools are converted into hospitals; the football field is changed into an observation clinic; and the crematorium is running on a round-the-clock schedule. The plague continues on its deathly path until January, and then it departs almost as mysteriously as it came.

The people of Oran react to the plague in various ways. Many are passive, for they continue to live their day to day lives almost unperturbed. They go to the cafes and movies. Some take refuge in religion, but as the disease persists their interest tends to wane. A few take advantage of the stricken city by blackmarketing goods that are scarce. In fact, some are even disappointed when the plague is over. Still there are others who are fighters. They work long hours with tireless energy trying to ward off this enemy which is bringing such human misery. Yet, one thing everyone has in common; one senses his exile from the remainder of the world; for they are completely cut off from friends and relatives outside the infected city. It is even impossible to mail letters for fear they too might spread the deadly infection.

As the story progresses, the question arises as to what exactly does Camus mean by the plague? It is doubtful that the obvious answer is the correct answer; that is, it is unlikely that the author is talking about a particular city that was hit by the bubonic plague. As the novel was originally published in 1947, some have interpreted the plague as representing the Nazi occupation of France during the Second World War. Although Camus might have had the occupation in mind, it seems to me that the plague can be legitimately interpreted in a more general way, having a more universal meaning. There is a sense in which we, as men and women living in the world, exist under the shadow of the plague. In other words, the plague might be a symbol for man's mortality. It may be seen as representing the hostility the universe is capable of inflicting on man. As such, it is expressed through disease, natural catastrophe, and death.

If we expand the symbolic meaning of the plague so as to include man's mortality, and especially those aspects of human existence which bring suffering, it is then possible to speak of three types of people. First, there are the infectors, namely those who may not suffer much themselves, but they carry the deadly virus so that they infect others and accelerate their mortal condition. Or, there are the true healers, who do everything within their power to prevent others from suffering and attempt to alleviate the suffering inflicted on others. Between these two broad extremes, there stand most people. What Camus is challenging us with is: if we cannot be true healers ourselves, can we try to avoid being pestilences?

The two characters whom we shall focus on are both

attempting to be true healers. The first is a priest,
Father Paneloux, who is a learned Jesuit scholar. Although
his role is not central, it is significant in considering the
problem of suffering. During the plague, there is a very
important change that takes place in Paneloux. In the beginning, he is quite certain the people's wickedness is responsible for the epidemic, but as he works with the "sani-
tation squad," that is, the group responsible for moving the
corpses to the crematorium, his attitude changes. His change
is the result of observing the death of a small innocent child.

The change in the priest can be seen by an examination
of his sermons. During the plague two of his sermons are
reported. At the beginning he preaches a sermon to a large
congregation. Many had come because they were curious as to
how a man of God might interpret their situation. Seeing the
large body of people and instinctively knowing their anxiety,
he took advantage of the moment. In other words, he was too
eager to exploit their fear of the plague to get them to turn
to the church. At one point in his first sermon Paneloux
says:

> If today the plague is in your midst, that is because
> the hour has struck for taking thought. The just man
> need have no fear, but the evildoer has good cause to
> tremble. For plague is the flail of God and the world
> His threshing-floor, and implacably He will thresh out
> His harvest until the wheat is separated from the chaff.
> There shall be more chaff than wheat, few chosen of the
> many called. Yet this calamity was not willed by God.
> Too long this world of ours has connived at evil, too
> long has it counted on the divine mercy, on God's forgive-
> ness. Repentance was enough men thought; nothing was

forbidden. Everyone felt comfortably assured; when the
day came, he would surely turn from his sins and repent.
Pending that day, the easiest course was to surrender
all along the line; divine compassion would do the rest.
For a long while God gazed down on this town with eyes
of compassion; but He grew weary of waiting, His eternal
hope was too long deferred, and now He has turned His
face away from us. And so, God's light withdrawn, we
walk in darkness, in the thick darkness of the plague.[1]

After Paneloux drives home the idea that the plague is the

result of the people's wickedness, he concludes his sermon

by exhorting his congregation to return to God in prayer.

And then he says God will do the rest, implying the righteous

will be saved from the plague.

Between Paneloux's first sermon and his second one,

several months transpire, and during this interim the plague

picks up momentum. At one point both Father Paneloux and

Dr. Rieux stand by the bedside of an innocent child, as he

unsuccessfully attempts to fight off the disease. In dis-

cussing the child's death with the priest Dr. Rieux says:

"Ah! That child, anyhow, was innocent, and you know it as

well as I do!" Later in the conversation, the priest speaks

in a low voice: "I understand...That sort of thing is revolt-

ing because it passes our human understanding. But perhaps

we should love what we cannot understand." Trying to over-

come his weariness, Rieux shakes his head and replies:

"No, Father, I've a very different idea of love. And
until my dying day I shall refuse to love a scheme of
things in which children are put to torture..."
Paneloux sat down beside Rieux. It was obvious that

_____

[1]Ibid., pp. 87-88.

he was deeply moved.

"Yes, yes," he said, "you, too, are working for man's salvation."

"Salvation's much too big a word for me. I don't aim so high. I'm concerned with man's health; and for me his health comes first."[1]

Not long after the death of the child, Paneloux gave his second sermon. This time the church was nearly empty, being a mass especially for men. Because the priest had personally invited the doctor, Rieux was present. Paneloux began his sermon by stating that trials, regardless of how cruel they may appear, work together for the good of the Christian. The problem for the man of faith is to discern the good in his hour of trial and to use the discernment to strengthen himself so that he might successfully endure the suffering. What was needed was to discern what the plague had to teach Oran. Believing discernment to be the problem, he now proceeds to point out what he believes the plague is teaching them. He sees it as a time of testing. It is a time in which people must either believe everything or they must deny everything. There is no middle way. Thus the religion that must deal with the plague is not the everyday religion practiced by most people. There are times to be light-hearted and joyful, but the present is not such a time. During the time of radical suffering God is placing great demands upon them. So they must practice the religion of all or they must practice the religion of nothing.

---

[1]Ibid., p. 197.

By contending the Christian must believe all, Paneloux
meant the Christian must accept everything, even the plague.
Acceptance in this context does not mean mere resignation,
nor humility, but it means a kind of humiliation in which the
person humiliated gives full assent to the destruction brought
on by the disease, including the death of an innocent child, or
even one's own death if such becomes the case. Since it was
God's will that an innocent child suffer, the Christian
must will it also. It is this way that the Christian comes
to the heart of the matter. The Christian comes to the place
where he must either believe everything or deny everything.
The person of faith must yield himself completely to the divine
will even the tragic deaths of thousands of people, and
"even though it passes his understanding." The time of the
plague is a radical time, with no possibility for a safe
middle ground. The individual must either love God or he
must hate God. The priest concludes his sermon with: "...
the love of God is a hard love. It demands total self-sur-
render, disdain of our human personality. And yet it alone
can reconcile us to suffering and the deaths of children,
it alone can justify them, since we cannot understand them,
and we can only make God's will ours."[1]

The title of Paneloux's sermon was "Is a Priest Justified
in Consulting a Doctor?" A few days after preaching this

---

[1] Ibid., p. 205.

sermon, he was granted the opportunity to put into practice what he preached, for the priest became ill. There is some question as how to interpret the priest's death. As it is not clear that he dies of the plague, some interpret it as the result of a man losing faith and dying in despair. However, I do not think this is a valid interpretation, for it would be a complete repudiation of the priest's recent sermon. I think the priest refused to call a doctor because he saw clearly the implications for his faith, regardless of how distorted his interpretation was. In other words, he died believing his death was the will of God. He simply refused to rebel against the divine will. By accepting his death, he gave his all to his Creator.

The priest tells his story about suffering from his understanding of the Christian story. However, this is not the only story told in The Plague, and from Camus' personal story, it is not the most important one. The doctor also has a story to tell, and he tells it from a different blik. So in order to fully understand Camus' understanding of the problem of suffering, we must listen to the story of the doctor.

Dr. Bernard Rieux is about thirty-five years of age, the son of a working man, who is now deceased. His sick wife went off to a sanitorium a few days before the plague begins, and she dies shortly before it ends. So the doctor is separated from his wife during the whole crisis. However, his mother remains with him as his housekeeper. The doctor is obviously the protagonist in the story although he does not reveal that it is he who is telling the whole story until the very end.

In one scene the doctor is talking with Tarrou. Tarrou is a stranger in town who was forced to remain because of the outbreak of the disease. He is a very sensitive person, and he is appointed as head of the "sanitary squad." As he and the doctor endure the plague together, they become the closest of friends. Tarrou asks the doctor why he entered the medical profession, and Rieux replies:

> I haven't a notion, Tarrou; I assure you I haven't a notion. When I entered the profession, I did it 'abstractly,' so to speak; because I had a desire for it, because it meant a career like another, one that young men often aspire to. Perhaps, too, because it was particularly difficult for a workman's son, like myself. And then I had to see people die. Do you know there are some people who refuse to die? Have you ever heard a woman scream "Never!" with her last gasp? Well, I have. And then I saw that I could never get hardened to it. I was young then, and I was outraged by the whole scheme of things, or so I thought. Subsequently I grew more modest. Only, I've never managed to get used to seeing people die. That's all I know...[1]

And then Rieux continues:

> ...its something that a man of your sort can understand most likely, but, since the order of the world is shaped by death, mightn't it be better for God if we refused to believe in Him and struggle with all our might against death, without raising our eyes toward heaven where he sits in silence.'
> Tarrou nodded.
> "Yes, but your victories will never be lasting that's all.'

---

[1] Ibid., p. 117.

Rieux's face darkened.

'Yes, I know that. But it's no reason for giving up the struggle.'

'No reason, I agree. Only, I now can picture what this plague must mean for you.'

'Yes. A never ending defeat.'

Tarrou asks Rieux directly:

'Do you believe in God, doctor?'

Again the question was put in an ordinary tone. But this time Rieux took longer to find his answer.

'No--but what does that really mean? I'm fumbling in the dark, struggling to make something out. But I've long ceased finding that original.'

'...My question's this,' said Tarrou. 'Why do you yourself show such devotion, considering you don't believe in God? I suspect your answer may help me to mine.'

His face still in shadow, Rieux said that he'd already answered: that if he believed in an all-powerful God he would cease curing the sick and leave that to Him. But no one in the world believed in a God of that sort; no, not even Paneloux, who believed that he believed in such a God. And that this was proved by the fact that no one ever threw himself on Providence completely. Anyhow, in this respect Rieux believed himself to be on the right road--in fighting against creation as he found it. [1]

Dr. Rieux then does not believe in God. This does not mean that he is anti-Christian; it simply implies that for him the question of God is irrelevant because it does not change the conditions in the world. He therefore lives in a world where God is absent. In his world people are born, they live, they die. His place in the world is to fight against disease and to keep people alive as long as is humanly possible. He realizes that ultimately this is a futile fight since all men eventually must die, but he is trying to prolong life and keep away the "death angel." His fighting the plague

---

[1] Ibid., p. 116.

is motivated by "common decency" and "just doing his job."
It is what any doctor should do. Rieux feels that he is in
the same boat with all men, for he feels a common identity
with them. He knows that even if the epidemic is stopped,
the "plague" will eventually get him, whether today or tomorrow or thirty years hence. He therefore rebels against
the finitude of man although he realizes that he is plagued
by the same finitude.

The story of the doctor most closely represents Camus'
point of view. He believes we live in an indifferent and
uncaring universe. In this life man is confronted with evil
which causes suffering. He advocates a position of moderation,
that is, to avoid falling into a nihilism whose logic can
lead to suicide and to avoid jumping into the Christian faith
which is more absurd than man's experience of suffering.
For Camus, Sisyphus is the paradigm for man. Being punished
by the gods, he is forced to eternally push a heavy stone up
an incline, with it rolling down again just as the peak appears to be obtainable. So man rebels against evil, knowing
that when he conquers it in one time and place it will crop
up again. Yet, it is man standing alone and joining with his
compatriots in trying to drive evil and suffering out of the
universe that gives life its limited meaning.

3. Conclusion

For both MacLeish and Camus, the presence of suffering in the world is real. It must be taken seriously, for it overshadows everything man does. Both writers come to a humanist, not a Christian conclusion; namely, man is alone in an indifferent universe and must live his life within the parameters set by birth and death.

The Christian must agree with these authors that suffering is indeed real. He knows that some people are so overwhelmed either by it or reflecting on it that religious faith is driven from their lives. Yet, for those who are capable of maintaining their faith in the face of suffering and evil, the stories of MacLeish and Camus, though honest and moving, are not sufficient. They have limited their view of reality to this world and to an isolated view of man. For the Christian, they are correct as far as they go, but they do not go far enough. Beyond this empirical world there is the dimension of the spirit, and standing both behind and within the human drama there is the divine Creator who cares about his creation.

In the Christian story suffering was not an original part of existence. It came into the world as a result of man's turning away from the source of his being and listening to the serpent. When man alienated himself from the ground of his being, his fall not only affected him, it had a cosmic significance. Suffering then is the result of the original

alienation from God. Obviously some suffering is the outcome
of man living in his alienated state. This is seen in the
genocide program of the Nazis against the Jews or the suffering resulting from war against nations. However, the
suffering resulting from nature, such as tornadoes, the
eruption of volcanoes, and earthquakes, is the consequence
of the disruption that came into the world through the original fall of man. As MacLeish and Camus both point out,
there need be no necessary connection between an individual's
personal sin and his personal suffering, for much suffering
is the outcome of being born into a world that has already
been disrupted and run by human beings who are sons of Adam.

We take issue with Paneloux; namely, this does not imply
that the Christian should not try to set the world right,
to join with the humanist in fighting against evil, to take
the world and its suffering seriously. However, the Christian
now knows that suffering can never completely be abolished
in this life. At most it can only be reduced, and the Christian believes that this can best be achieved by men of talent
being reconciled to God and then with the gift of divine
grace going out into the world and trying to change it.
As both the Christian and the non-Christian are forced to
live in an alienated and disrupted world, they are limited
in what they can accomplish.

As we look back over this chapter, we do not claim
that we have solved the problem of suffering. We have not,

but neither have we ignored it, for at the present time, it is perhaps unsolvable from the Christian perspective. Yet, we have placed the problem within the Christian story, which means that any adequate explanation must take into account the transcendental dimension of reality, the estrangement of man from the source of his being, and the suffering of Christ on the cross.

In the early 1960's, the brilliant Jewish theologian, the late Abraham Heschel, gave a public lecture at Brown University. Following the lecture, some faculty and graduate students met with the speaker to discuss his presentation. At the small gathering, I raised the problem of suffering with Heschel. I phrased it this way: "Professor Heschel, there are stories in the Bible where people call upon God, and he answers their prayers. He answered Elijah's prayer at Mount Carmel. I would imagine that millions of Jews prayed to God for deliverance from the gas chambers of the Nazis. Why do you think God did not deliver them?" Dr. Heschel's response was: "No question has ever disturbed me more than this one. I have struggled with it for a long time. But I will not give in to skepticism. I can only say with Job that the ways of God are not the ways of man, and though God slay me still I shall worship him!"

CHAPTER VI

DEATH

Examining the human condition from the context of the Christian story, we have seen that as a result of man's rebellion and subsequent alienation from God, he has disoriented himself in the world. In this fallen state, man is a sinner and he experiences suffering. As we continue our examination, we shall deal with the final major characteristic of the human condition, which is death. As is the case with sin and suffering, death characterizes man's existence after the fall, so in some sense it is connected with the original rebellion in paradise.

From the perspective of the Christian story, there is a kind of ambiguity about death. The ambiguity stems from the fact that the term applies to both the death of the body and also to the death of the "spirit" or personality. The first kind of death gives us the least trouble, for it comes when life ceases to function in the biological organism. It is the kind of death that is currently debated about in medical journals as to whether a person is dead when his brain ceases to function or when his heart stops beating. It is often associated with corpses, funeral directors, and expensive burials. This kind of death is the antithesis of life of the

body. People who walk around on the streets are considered
to be biologically and medically alive. Physical life then
is bounded on one side by birth and on the other by death.
We therefore can be either physically alive or physically
dead, but we cannot be both at the same time.

But man not only dies physically; he can also die spiritually. This second kind of death is much more difficult to
understand or pin down. It deals with the death of the person
rather than the death of the body. In other words, the
Christian story says it is possible for a person to be physically alive, but to be dead as a human being. Hence it is
possible to be walking around in a live body but to be in-
wardly dead. When we are dead as persons, we are no longer
fully human, but we have become animals.

Two contemporary playwrights, who have been interested
in this problem, are Tennessee Williams, the American playwright and Eugene Ionesco, the French dramatist. We shall
therefore use their plays as modern versions of the issues
raised biblically. Since death, in the Christian context,
carries a double meaning, we shall look at two works which
focus on physical death and two which look at the more illusive
spiritual death.

1. Picking Up Carcasses From The Street

Tennessee Williams' Camino Real[1] drives home the fact

---

[1](New York: New Directions, 1953).

that man is going to die. Some people are shocked and re-
pelled by Williams' drama, but if we look behind his excesses,
we might well discover that he is struggling with problems
that are very near to us. We therefore must not allow his
excesses and exaggerations to drive us away from the real
issues he is raising. This is especially the case with his
handling of the subject of death.

Camino Real, though it was produced several years before
MacLeish's J. B., has a similar structure. This is to say,
there are no acts as such, but rather the drama begins with
a prologue and moves through sixteen scenes, referred to
as "blocks" on the Camino Real. The action takes place in
some unspecified Latin-American country, in a village at the
end of nowhere.

Williams maintains that all men travel on the Camino
Real. For to be on the king's highway is to be a human being
living in the world. The Camino Real is walled-in with a
number of deadend streets. There is only one exit, and
Williams refers to it as the "Terra Incongnita." But his
characters never have the courage to move through the exit
into this unknown land. Occasionally, there are unexpected
plane flights in and out of Camino Real. Everyone desperately
attempts to board the plane; but because they do not have the
proper passports, or the correct currency, or for some other
trivial reason, they are never able to escape. The unknown
flights seem to represent man's hope for the miraculous.

Some miraculous thing will happen in the world that will
enable him to escape from the world and his certain death;
but in Williams' scheme of things, the miraculous never
really happens.

Like in real life, people who travel the king's highway
are either rich or poor or are living on the wealth of another.
So life is an entrance and an exit; you enter into it and you
exit out of it. While you are between the entrance and the
exit you are plagued by the fear of death and anxiety about
the unknown time of its arrival. With money you can endure
your anxiety about death in affluent surroundings, but without
it you must suffer your anxiety in poverty. Whether rich
or poor, man is harassed by the same anxiety.

The omni-presence of death is symbolized in the street
cleaners, who are attired in little white jackets somewhat
like orderlies in a hospital. They stand around like vultures
waiting for someone to die. When the inevitable happens, they
pile the corpse up in a trash barrel not unlike a garbage
can and cart it away. They smile cynically and point their
fingers at people traveling on the highway. Everyone knows
that eventually the street cleaners will pick his carcass
up from the streets. Yet, a genuine anxiety exists because
no one can be sure when his number is up.

Of course, in this drama written before Williams converted to Roman Catholicism, the author is attempting to make
us accept the fact that we are going to die. Although life

for him at that time appearedtobeultimately tragic, he indicates it is possible to establish a kind of short-lived
"love" relationship, for the character, Qui ote, says at the
end: "The violets in the mountains have broken the rocks!"[1]
having reference to a conversation between two other characters, Marguerite and Jacques, when the latter suggests that
love is their only defense for coping with their condition.
In the conversation Marguerite thinks that love is about as
possible as it is for violets in the mountains to break the
rocks.[2] It is true that this love might be immature and
egocentric, but because of the finitude of man, such experiences take on a significant meaning.

In the Camino Real Williams has a blik that is nearer
that of MacLeish and Camus than it is to the Christian story.
In it there is neither a loving, caring Creator, nor any
hope of eternal life implied. Man is simply an animal who
knows that he will die and this knowledge creates a kind of
anxiety that incapacitates him. The life of man is lived
from the context of a cold, indifferent universe, and his
fate is death. Williams' man does not even have the courage
to rebel as did Camus' Dr. Rieux. At most, in an egotistic
way, man can attempt to love, but even then he cannot be very
successful.

---

[1]Ibid., p. 161.

[2]Ibid., p. 97.

2. <u>The Killer Is Ubiquitous</u>

In many respects Ionesco shares the vision of Williams.
It comes through in many of his works, especially in his very
well-known <u>Exit The King</u> and his not so well-known <u>The
Killer</u>.[1] For our purposes, we shall examine the latter.
<u>The Killer</u> is a three act play whose action takes place in a
city like Paris. The action begins with Berenger, who is the
protagonist in at least four of Ionesco's plays, and who is
a kind of middle-class symbol of Everyman, being shown through
the exclusive section of the city by an architect. In con-
trast to the cold dampness of his present residence, the new
city is a "radiant city," "a smiling city," where the houses
are extremely well built and even the climate is ideally
controlled. As they move from one street to the next, their
conversation is interrupted by telephone calls to the architect who has a portable phone in his pocket.

The Everyman character of Berenger is revealed through a
conversation about his age, for he might be thirty-five,
or even one-hundred-twenty. Also, it is not clear how one
reaches the "radiant city," for Berenger explains that his
arrival was like successfully finding one's way through a
very complicated maze. In fact, he says he reached it by
"pure accident." This ideal spot is like a "mirage," but
as the blazing fire which he possessed as a youth has gone

---

[1](New York: Grove Press, 1960), tr. by Donald Watson.

out, he feels a need for a change of environment.[1]

Entering his office, the architect receives another
phone call, and he takes care of the telephone with one eye
and one ear and carries on his conversation with Berenger
with his other eye and ear. Berenger explains how there have
been moments in his life which have revived his life force.
The last time was when he was eighteen, walking down a street
in a city in southern France. He heard no sounds, but he
recalls the sun was brilliant. All of a sudden he experienced
a kind of purity and fulfillment. The experience did not last
long, as the everydayness of the day returned: noise, a
regular sky, and people crying. In the midst of all this,
he felt very much alone. While Berenger told his story,
the architect tries to follow it and keep up a conversation
on the phone with his secretary who is trying to resign her
job. Although he has never repeated this experience, the memory
of it gives him a reason to go on living. But as the memory
is beginning to fade, Berenger thinks the radiant city might
restore his zest for living.

If this city can restore his zest for living, Berenger
might even be able to love again. Just as he says this,
Dany, the architect's secretary arrives and tells Berenger
she will have to think about it. A rather comical conversation begins with Dany trying to carry on two separate

---

[1]Ibid., p. 20.

conversations with the two men. She tells the architect she is quitting her job and that he will be unable to dissuade her, while Berenger tries to persuade her to marry him and live with him in the radiant city. Without receiving an answer, Dany runs out in a huff because of her irritation with her boss, and Berenger informs the architect he will buy the white house which is almost completed.

As they are talking a stone falls near Berenger, and they hear the sound of broken window panes. Yet, the city streets are completely deserted without the slightest signs of life. Other stones are thrown, and then the architect informs Berenger that the police have suspended all construction; hence his house will not be completed. He explains that no one wishes to buy property in the district now and that actually the people wish to move and would do so if there were houses available to them elsewhere. The local inhabitants remain secretly hidden in their homes, and they only come out when there are large numbers together. Of course, Berenger raises the question why. It is then that the architect explains that the people are being killed and shows him a swimming pool where three bodies are presently floating. Almost every day there are new bodies in the pool. Berenger's inner glow begins to die as he realizes the radiant city is not all it is cracked up to be. There is a very elusive murderer in the district. When Berenger hears this, he wishes to leave immediately, but the architect comforts him by explaining that he is also a civil servant and that Berenger will not be harmed as long as he is with him.

Discovering there is no radiant city has a devastating effect on Berenger, for he concludes there is no point in living. However, the architect confides to him that he is also the chief of police and he hopes to catch the killer before he retires. He escorts Berenger to the subway entrance, from which he can return home. While they are waiting for the next train, they decide to have a drink at a bar next door, which happens to be across from a cemetery. By now the weather has changed; an icy rain is falling and grayness has overtaken the bright radiance. After they have entered the bar and been seated at a table, the architect tries to cheer his companion up. He says: "If we thought of all the misfortunes of mankind, we could not go on living. And we must live!...In the end it's the bright side you've got to bear in mind."[1] Berenger admits that he is physically and mentally in good shape; what is disturbing him is not visible; "it's theoretical, spiritual."[2]

Revelations about the architect continue. He explains he is not only chief of police, but he is a physician who has known of others with Berenger's malady. After the owner has rid the bar of a drunken Clackard, he serves the men their drinks. The architect tells Berenger that he has a description

---

[1] Ibid., p. 36.

[2] Ibid., p. 37.

of the Killer and how he strikes. He explains that the Killer comes to the train stop and pretends to be a beggar, selling cheap articles. He stays with a passenger until he or she reaches the pool. He then suggests showing them a photograph of the Colonel, which is irresistible. Since looking at the picture is a very engrossing and disturbing experience, he pushes the victim into the pool, where he drowns. As soon as he has finished off one victim, he goes in search of another. Although the people in the radiant city have been informed as to how the Killer operates, they are still taken in by him. Even police have been murdered in the same fashion. As they discuss the murderous fiend, they look out the window, seeing the commuters as they file out on the street. As they watch, they hear a dreadful scream, and the sound of someone striking the water. Berenger jumps up from the table demanding they do something at once, but the architect continues to calmly munch on his sandwich acknowledging he has been outsmarted again. The owner of the bar comes to the table and tells them the victim was Dany, his ex-secretary and the woman Berenger asked to marry him. The architect telephones the report into the office in a matter-of-fact sort of way, while Berenger goes into a state of hysteria, demanding that something be done. The first act ends with him running frantically out of the bar, while the architect remains at the table calmly taking another bite from his sandwich.

The second act begins outside Berenger's apartment

building, where people are going about their everyday, mundane activities and conversations. The postman comes to the building to deliver a telegram to Berenger, but he is not at home. So the cleaning woman agrees to deliver it. When he returns shortly, the telegram is given to him and he goes to his apartment, where he finds Edouard, a man with a deformed hand waiting. Berenger tells his visitor that he is in despair and inconsolable because of the sudden murder of his girl friend, Dany. Noting he had found the radiant city, he explains it has lost its appeal because "a criminal, an insatiable murderer, has turned it into a hell."[1] When Edouard informs him that he knows all about the story, even telling about how the Killer uses the Colonel's photograph to lure his victims to the pool, Berenger is most surprised. In fact, Edouard confides that the whole town knows the story. His calmness and general acceptance of the situation, like that of the architect, infuriates Berenger.

Edouard has a terrible cough, so he asks Berenger to go for a walk with him to get some fresh air. As they stand to depart, Edouard strikes his large black briefcase against a table, releasing the catch so that the contents fall on the floor. Much to Berenger's amazement, numerous photographs of the Colonel with his many decorations and Military Cross are among the mess. There also are dirty pictures and a

---

[1]Ibid., p. 63.

heterogeneous collection of articles, which the owner could not explain. Berenger realizes immediately that they are the Killer's objects; and among them, there is a calling card with the Killer's name and address on it. Also, there is a diary with a list of the victims, and a detailed confession of how and when he murdered them. With such damaging evidence, Berenger becomes ecstatic, for he believes it is now possible to catch the Killer and prosecute him.

When Edouard is questioned about how the materials came into his possession, he explains that the Killer gave them to him requesting they be published in a literary journal. However, Edouard did not take them seriously, for they appeared to him like idle dreams of no importance. Yet, Berenger feels that if he had taken them seriously, the murders might have been prevented. Until he pointed out the connection between the documents and the real murders, Edouard had not been able to make it. With the two determined to take the incriminating documents to the police, they rush out of the apartment, forgetting the briefcase with the all-important materials lying on the floor.

The third act begins with Mother Peep giving a sidewalk political speech. Members of the crowd shout: "Long live Mother Peep's geese!" En route to the police station, the two men pass the political rally. Being exhausted from hurrying, Edouard is forced to stop for a short rest. With the political rally continuing in the background, Berenger notices his companion does not have the briefcase. They begin to search frantically for it realizing the police will not take them seriously without the evidence. As Berenger looks, he sees an inebriated man, standing with a briefcase. Believing it is Edouard's, he attempts to take it from the drunk. When the case is opened, they see it belongs to the man as there is only a bottle of wine in it.

Next a little old man with a briefcase arrives on the scene asking directions to the Danube. With Mother Peep conducting her political rally in the background, Edouard and Berenger take the briefcase and examine it but discover it is not theirs. By now the political mob has become excited and start to do the goose-step. The drunk challenges Mother Peep, arguing that scientists and artists have done more to change the world than politicians. A fight begins, and Berenger sees amid all the commotion that Mother Peep herself has a briefcase. He grabs it and hits a man over the head with it. The briefcase opens and the contents fall to the ground. There is only the "goose game."

A policeman arrives and disperses the crowd. While he is doing his work, two military trucks drive up. Berenger informs the old man that he is looking for a briefcase containing important documents. The old man suggests that he left it at his home. When Berenger asked him how he knew, the old man replies it was just simple deduction. Edouard returns to the apartment, while Berenger rushes to the police station hoping to hold them until the documents have arrived. However, the military trucks have created a traffic jam, and Berenger is pushed aside and delayed by a policeman. After he produces his identification papers, the traffic jam miraculously disappears, i.e., the police, the army, and the crowd. All of a sudden Berenger finds himself alone, and he goes into a state of fright.

With the streets deserted, Berenger rushes to the police station with a growing sense of anxiety. As he runs, he wonders whether the station will be closed, will Edouard arrive with the briefcase, and will it make any difference whether he makes his report today or tomorrow. Finally deciding he will wait until tomorrow to submit his report, he looks down the empty street and sees the Killer. He is a small, puny, ill-shaven man with a derisive laugh and has one eye. It is not clear whether the Killer is actually there or whether Berenger is hallucinating. As the Killer comes nearer with his continuous idiotic laugh, Berenger notes that he, himself, is much larger and stronger than the murderer. In fact, he senses that he is no longer afraid of him. When Berenger tries to get the Killer to explain to him why he kills, he simply shrugs his shoulders and laughs. Berenger tells the Killer that because of his murdering he has brought unhappiness to him and to many others. He has taken all the radiance out of life. Berenger suggests various reasons as to why the Killer commits his crimes, but the Killer does

not respond to any of them. Finally, the Killer takes out a
shiny knife, but Berenger responds by taking two pistols
from his pockets and aims them at his adversary. However,
as the fiend approaches, he does not have a strong enough
will to pull the triggers. So Berenger drops his weapons to
the ground, falls on his knees, as the chuckling, ugly dwarf
comes closer with his knife. Berenger cries out: "Oh God!
there's nothing we can do. What can we do...What can we do..."
The play ends with Everyman's cry of desperation as inevitable
death approaches.

As did Williams, Ionesco has vividly driven home the
fact that man is mortal, that he is going to die. The Killer
stalks Everyman and ultimately he will meet him on the lonely,
deserted street and have his way. Emotional outbursts, nor
rational arguments, nor crying out to the high heavens can
or will alter this fact. Just as Berenger tried, we too can
move from the less affluent and less beautiful sections of
the city to the radiant city itself, but we cannot escape
the ugly, idiotic, laughing dwarf always coming just one
step closer. Because there is no escape, we cannot find the
kind of happiness and contentment we most desire. In fact,
we can become so aware and so threatened by the ugly, devilish
Killer that we cease to be alive as human beings. We can
become so crippled by the threat of physical death that we

---

[1]Ibid., p. 109.

die as people. Berenger admits that this is exactly what has happened to him. He says: "a force...it must have been the life force...And then it grew weaker and all died away."[1]

So behind the official functions of institutions, the political rhetoric of parties, the creative work of artists and scientists, the labor and meaningless chatter of the common man, there is the Killer. In the face of inevitable death, it is difficult to take these institutions and concerns too seriously. They will continue with their functions carried out by those who come after us, but we shall not and this is where the tragedy and meaninglessness of existence lies. As Berenger tries to argue with the Killer, he says:

> Listen I'm going to make you a painful confession. Often, I have my doubts about everything too. But don't tell anyone. I doubt the point of living, the meaning of life, doubt my own values and every kind of rational argument. I no longer know what to hang on to, perhaps there's no more truth or charity. But if that's the case, be philosophical; if all is vanity, if charity is vanity, crime's just vanity too . . . When you know everything's dust and ashes, you'd be a fool if you set any store by crime, for that would be setting store by life . . . That would mean you were taking things seriously . . . There's nothing worse than being stupid.[2]

3. Man Is A Beetle

The death of the body is an aspect of human existence which cannot be avoided, but, as we noted earlier, there is a second kind of death. There is the death of the "spirit"

---

[1] Ibid., p. 20.

[2] Ibid., p. 106.

or personality. This kind of death is the result of man's radical estrangement from the source of his being. In his alienation, sin, suffering, and physical death, the human being becomes so intimidated by these powers that he or she loses the capacity to be truly human. Yet, there is a sense in which man has some control over this second death, namely, to become reconciled to his Creator. But we shall forego a discussion of this until the next chapter. The point in this second type of death also has been depicted by literary artists in a variety of ways. One method is to focus on the trans-formation of man from a human being to some kind of an animal. Both Franz Kafka and Eugene Ionesco have done this success-fully. So we shall look at the stories they tell about the death of the personality.

Franz Kafka, one of the truly great literary figures of Czechoslovakia, has touched on our problem in an intriguing and powerful short story entitled The Metamorphosis.[1] In this story, Gregor Samsa is an only son who lives with his parents and unmarried sister. He is a successful traveling salesman, who is responsible for supporting his family which he does quite adequately. One morning Gregor awakes, and much to his dismay, discovers that he has turned into a gigantic insect, having the appearance somewhat like that of a beetle. Because of the extreme difficulty involved in just getting

---

[1] Selected Stories of Franz Kafka (New York: Modern Library, 1952), tr. by Willa and Edwin Muir, pp. 19-89.

out of bed, he becomes worried about missing his train and not arriving at his job on time. His anxiety is not in vain. When he does not arrive at his office, his supervisor comes out to his house to check on him, but he leaves immediately because of the chaos in the Samsa household, resulting from the metamorphosis. Although the family is somewhat disturbed that their breadwinner has changed into an insect-looking creature, they are confident that his condition is only temporary and that eventually he will return to his normal self.

Gregor's sister accepts the responsibility for feeding him, but since his change, he no longer appreciates the taste of human food. In time he so withdraws from the various members of his family that he no longer can communicate with them. He remains alone in his room, isolated from the other members of the household. Occasionally he walks around on the ceiling somewhat like a fly as this was a comfortable position for him. As the financial situation of the Samsas worsens, first the father goes and then the sister tries to gain employment, but both are unsuccessful. Without a source of income, the domestic help is released. Finally, three young boarders are taken in to help with the finances, but they depart when Gregor frightens them out of their wits. One day the father becomes angry with his son and throws apples at him as he holds on to the ceiling. The wounds received from the apples are so severe that poor Gregor dies.

As we read the story, we sense the isolation and alienation of Gregor from other human beings. It becomes increasingly impossible for him to relate meaningfully to the other members of his family. Yet, despite the fact that the metamorphosis has taken place, at one point Gregor raises the question: "Am I less sensitive now?"

Although his story is most unusual, Kafka's message is rather obvious. Gregor Samsa is his symbol for the modern middle-class man, living in an industrial society. He is a man who seems to be doing all right in the world. Gregor gets up in the morning, takes his train, goes to work, returns home, and later goes to bed. He does exactly the same thing year in and year out, having gotten himself into a deep rut. He has become so depersonalized by his monotonous job in our modern industrial society that he is no longer a human being, but he has become an ugly insect devoid of personality and the ability to enter into meaningful relationships with other human beings, even his family. His life has become dull and spiritless, and the result has a severe adverse effect on him as symbolized by the gigantic beetle he has become. Or to put it another way, Gregor Samsa was physically alive, but he was dead as a person.

4. Infectious Rhinoceritis

Eugene Ionesco is also interested in the problem of man losing his humanity and becoming an animal. He deals with it overtly in his unusual and significant play,

Rhinoceros,[1] which was written in the late fifties and established the author as a major figure in the theatre.
The original idea for the play dates back to the late thirties,
when Ionesco found himself in Rumania, the native country of
his father. Everyone around him was accepting without criticism
the Nazi propaganda, and he remembers how out of place and
alone he felt in the midst of this mass hysteria. So he
recaptures much of that feeling in Rhinoceros.

The action of the play unfolds in three acts. Again,
Berenger is the protagonist, who immediately confesses that
he does not feel at home in the world. He does not feel
comfortable when he is alone; and then when he joins with
others, he still does not. Yet, there is a sense in which
he takes life in its stride and lives it in his eccentric
authentic sort of way.

On a typical Sunday morning, Berenger meets with his
friend, Jean, in a kind of sidewalk cafe in his average
provincial town. As Jean is criticizing him for his care-
less appearance, a rhinoceros runs through the center of
town. As the shop-keeper, his wife, an elderly gentleman,
and other solid citizens respond to the appearance of the
rhino, they make stupid, boring comments. Eventually they
get into a heated argument about whether an African or an
Asian rhinoceros has one or two horns. Without knowing which

---

[1](New York: Grove Press, 1960), tr. by Derek Prouse.

had one horn and which had two horns, some argue that the
rhino which ran through the town was African, whereas others
were equally certain it was Asian.

On the following Monday morning Berenger goes to work
as usual at the government office where he is a petty office
employee. As he arrives, he finds his fellow employees
furiously discussing the appearance of the rhino in the town
yesterday. Botard, an ex-school teacher and generally a
skeptic, doubts that anyone actually saw a rhinoceros run
through the town. In time Mr. Papillon, the office manager,
who represents a kind of exaggerated efficiency, gets the
office to settle down. But just as he thinks he has things
under control, the wife of an absent employee bursts into
the office to explain about her husband's absence and how
she was chased all the way to the office by a huge, ugly
rhino. When they hear a noise at the bottom of the stairs,
the workers go to see what is causing it, and they find a
rhinoceros which has an uncanny resemblance to the woman's
absent husband. Being a faithful and devoted wife, she
jumps on the animal's back and they leave in the direction
of their home.

Later in the day, Berenger goes to Jean's apartment to
apologize about their argument on Sunday. As Berenger carries
on a conversation with Jean, we see before our very eyes the
transformation of a man into a rhinoceros. At first Berenger
notices that Jean is rather hoarse, but Jean insists that he

is all right. Berenger then observes that Jean is beginning
to turn green, his skin is becoming like a tough hide, and a
bump is beginning to appear on his forehead. In a very short
time Jean is a rhino. Berenger becomes frightened and looks
out of the apartment window, discovering that the street
below is full of rhinos.

Leaving Jean's apartment, he rushes to his own, and
Dudard, a worker in his office, arrives. Both men are very
concerned about what is happening in their town. As they
are discussing the situation, Daisy, a friend of Berenger's
who also works in the office, runs into the apartment. We
learn from her that nearly everyone in the office has turned
into rhinos except these three. Even Mr. Papillon, the office
manager, and Botard, the skeptic, have turned. Shortly
Dudard leaves so that Berenger and Daisy might be alone;
but, as he departs, he becomes a rhinoceros. Now both Daisy
and Berenger fear that they too might become rhinos, for they
appear to be the only two human beings left. However, Berenger
believes that if they have love and courage, they might be
able to withstand the dreadful infection of rhinoceritis.

As the end of the play nears, Berenger looks at the
herd of rhinos and concludes: "They've all gone mad. The
world is sick. They're all sick." Then Berenger says:
"Listen, Daisy, there is something we can do. We'll have
children, and our children will have children--it'll take time,
but together we can regenerate the human race." Daisy

replies: "Regenerate the human race?" Berenger answers:
"It happened once before." Daisy: "Ages ago. Adam and
Eve...they had a lot of courage." Berenger insists: "And
we, too, can have courage. We don't need all that much.
It happens automatically with time and patience." Daisy
asks: "What's the use?" Berenger insists: "Of course we
can--with a little bit of courage." Daisy says frankly:
"I don't want to have children--it's a bore." Berenger then
asks: "How can we save the world, if you don't?" Daisy:
"Why bother to save it?"[1]

Like the rest, Daisy lacked the conviction to endure
being different from the majority. When she leaves Berenger's
apartment, she too becomes a huge insensitive beast. Berenger
is now alone, against the world and its herd of rhinos.
Yet, at the last minute, he thinks that he also would like to
become a beast; but he has been human far too long. Now
even if he wants to, he cannot become a rhino. He is stuck
with his humanity, and so he has to resign himself to it.
He is left as one human being in a world of huge, insensitive, conforming rhinoceroses.

The implication of Ionesco's is not too difficult to
see, for we are very much aware that a great deal of pressure
is placed upon modern men and women to become beasts and to
lose their fundamental humanity. Ionesco vividly points out

---

[1]Ibid., pp. 102-103.

why various people become rhinos. There are those who become members of the herd because they admire the brute force of the beast. There are others who say that if they are going to win back the herd for humanity, they must learn the way of thinking of the rhino, and then they can cautiously bring them back. But often the herd converts this person and we never hear from him again. Others will contend that you must move with the times, and if being rhinoceroses is in vogue, then you had best get on the bandwagon. Still others maintain that they cannot stand the pressure of being different from the majority; it is too strenuous being a man in a minority position. Thus, in Ionesco's play, we have everybody joining the herd, that is, the logician, the skeptic, the clergyman, the politician, and the solid citizen. As the play ends, being a rhinoceros is normal, but being a human being like Berenger is a monstrosity.

Ionesco seems to be saying that the person who makes decisions simply from pressures exerted from outside himself is less than a human being. Or to put the idea differently, the man who has lost the power to be himself is a rhinoceros. All of us are infected by rhinoceritis, but whether we are able to fight off the infection will depend upon our ability to withstand the pressures exerted upon us by society. For without some inward resources upon which to make valid ethical decisions, we are lost and do not know what decisions to make. We, therefore, finally end up watching the rhino on

our right and the one on our left, and we follow along with
the herd, believing that what we are doing is right because
the whole herd is doing it.

Of course, the difficulty is that often what the herd
is doing is not "right"; it is behaving a certain way out of
ignorance or prejudice, even though the herd may not realize
these are its real motivations. The herd of rhinoceroses
in Puritan New England thought that it was "right" to torture
so-called witches and dissenters to death; the herd of rhinoceroses in Nazi Germany thought it was "right" to exterminate
people simply because they happen to be Jews, and far too
many American rhinoceroses still today think that it is
"right" to discriminate against people because they happen
to have a dark skin color. Through the years pictures of
the herds in our large cities have been flashed on the television screens, protesting against equal rights for the black
man. When you see the hatred written all over their faces,
one cannot help but conclude they are not human beings, but
they are beasts.

But this is not the whole story. Ionesco implies in the
person of Berenger that it is possible for man to maintain
his humanity. In other words we do not have to move with
the herd, but rather we can be our particular expression of
Berenger. Or to put the idea in Christian terms, the man who
becomes reconciled to the source of his being will not be a
rhinoceros, but he will be a human being; he will be himself.

He will not be lost in the world, looking to the herd for his guidance, but he will have sufficient spiritual resources with which to make his own decisions, regardless of what the herd thinks.

Let us not misunderstand Ionesco at this point. He is not advocating that we become non-conformists for the sake of being different. No! Because it is even possible to conform to nonconformity. You will notice that Berenger is not the typical hero type. Often he does not fit in; he makes blunders and feels guilty when he does. Nor is he the crusader; nor is he beating the tin-tub in order to draw attention to himself. In fact, he does not appear to be a particularly strong leader at all. However, he does have some kind of inner strength. He has a conscience and he lives authentically. He is stuck with being himself, and he does not attempt to be somebody he is not.

5. Conclusion

In Camino Real and The Killer the reality of physical death has been brought vividly to our attention, and The Metamorphosis and Rhinoceros have portrayed some of the possibilities of existence in the face of physical extinction. In the presence of his certain death man can become an insect or an animal, forfeiting his humanity, or else he can retain his humanness as did Berenger.

The Christian story also affirms with Williams and Ionesco

the mortality of man, but it does not stop there. If this were the correct ending of the human story, it would be bleak indeed. But Christianity asserts that man was created by a God who cares, and this God raised Jesus from death to life. Just as divine love was exemplified in Jesus' death and resurrection, it will be present when the ugly, irrational Killer has done his job on the individual person. We do not know what the future life will be like, but we do know that God can be trusted and because of this man does not need to fear the future. As a result of the Christian's faith in the resurrection and its implications for his or her own future existence, death, as horrible as it might appear, can be endured without succumbing to the feeling of total meaninglessness.

Just as the Christian story affirms the reality of biological death as revealed by the literary artists, it also acknowledges the possibility of spiritual death. In fact, the Christian story maintains that it is the result of man's alienation from the creative power in the universe. In order for man to withstand the demonic powers in the world which seek to deprive him of his humanity, he must be reconciled to the ultimate power from which he has been alienated. The Christian asserts that reconciliation has been made possible by the Christ-event, as finalized in the death and resurrection of Jesus. So the Christ-event is the answer to both the problems of biological and spiritual death.

Looking now over the total scope of the human condition,
we have described it with the categories of sin, suffering,
and death. We have attempted to show how much of the work
of the modern literary artists lends itself to our understanding of the human condition, using stories told in a contemporary idiom. Neither the categories of the Christian story,
nor those of the modern story teller are very pleasant. Yet,
in the midst of all the ugliness and bleakness there have
been brief glimpses of affirmation. Grandier refused to
accept an alleged crime for which he was not guilty. Mobius
was willing to sacrifice himself for the good of mankind.
Berenger was unable to become a rhinoceros. Likewise, the
Christian story offers hope and affirmation.

The belief of the Christian is that man is a sinner
and is alienated from his Creator, but through the Christ-
event, a way for reconciliation has been achieved. In this
life man can never return to his lost innocence in paradise.
However, he can return to the Creator and re-establish a
relationship with the life-giving power of the universe.
Man will still die, but death will lose its crippling effect
on him. Hence his attitude toward death will change, and
this change will enable him to face death courageously. In
the Christ-event, God raised Jesus from the grave. As a
result of this, although man will still die, death will not
have the final say. Death will provide the doorway for moving

into another dimension of life. Man will continue to experience suffering, but, through the Christ-event, he knows
that Jesus suffered long before him and was able to endure.
Likewise, regardless of what evil befalls him, he will be
able to courageously endure because he knows that God will
be with him as he was in Jesus.

Sin, suffering, and death are as real to the Christian
man or woman as they are to anyone else. They will still
sin, though sin has been overcome; they will still suffer,
though it cannot defeat them; they will still experience
death of the body, though they have been grafted into a new
life in Christ. The difference is that they have been given
a new life as people, and when they encounter these adver-
sities, they know they are temporary and they do not have
to face them alone. Knowing this makes a significant difference; for now they can open themselves confidently toward
the future and endure, not by their own power, but by a power
that comes to them in space and time though it is outside
of both.

CHAPTER VII

THE PARADIGM OF CHRIST

In the Christian story there are two ways for human beings to exist in the world. The Gospel of John refers to them as being born of the "flesh" and being born of the "spirit," or living in "darkness" and living in the "light." Sometimes the Christian applies the simple designation of an earlier evangelical era to man's existence and refers simply to being "lost" and being "saved." The man who is "saved" not only experiences eternal life in the future, but his existence in the world now is radically different. Likewise the man who is lost is lost not simply in the future but he is lost now as well.

In the contemporary and pluralistic world in which we are now living, there is much debate about how one moves from one state of existence to another. The answer one gives will obviously be determined by the kind of blik one has accepted and the type of stories one tells. Thus, the Christian maintains that the capacity to move from death into life is brought about by an act of God in Christ. With this fundamental tenet in mind, we first shall explore the two modes of existence making use of more neutral, contemporary categories; and second, we shall critically examine three

164

literary works which shed light on the dynamics of the trans-
formation experience, especially as it is related to the
paradigm of Christ.

1. Inauthentic and Authentic Existence

The human person who is in a state of alienation experiences anxiety. The anxiety has no specific object. It
is "free floating" being the result of the precariousness
of the human condition. This anxiety is difficult for the
person to endure. One way out, as we have seen in Metamorphosis is to completely give up one's humanness and with-
draw. Another way more commonly taken to escape the anxiety
is by losing oneself in the world. The person can become a
member of the "herd" if we use Erich Fromm's term, or the
"masses" if we choose Karl Jasper's, or the "they" if we
follow Martin Heidegger's designation. He can run with the
other rhinoceroses. Every person senses some pressure to
conform to the values of his or her professional, social,
and economic group. The group "calls" to the individual to
identify with it. The individual is ready to accept the
comfort such identity brings.

When one is in the group, he or she is expected to see
life from the group's perspective. The person must think
what it thinks, feel what it feels, act as it acts. Since
groups are only average, the person too must become average.
A member escapes the anxiety of living in the world by

accepting the questions of the group as the appropriate questions to be raised and by accepting the answers of the group as the proper answers for the questions. So it is when one member raises the group question, another supplies the group answer. Each looks approvingly at the other, for their prejudices have been confirmed. When one looks into the face of another human being, one sees either an enemy, who is not a member of the group, or an ally who is actually only the reflected image of him or herself. In fact, each member of the group has the same "face" with little or no individuality remaining. They have opted for an inauthentic existence as a way out of the anxiety of alienation. Inauthentic persons have lost the power to be themselves. They no longer know who they are, or what they "ought" to be doing in the world. They only know what the group says they are, and what the group demands they be doing.

However, the person who lives in the world inauthentically has the possibility before him of living authentically. To say that man can live authentically implies that man has the capacity for making contact with the Creative Power within the universe. This Power is not impersonal but personal. It can express itself through its will. It speaks to man; so that a man either living inauthentically or being tempted to do so is called by this Creative Power. Of course, the individual can refuse to listen to the divine "call." For at the same time, the "call" of the group is tempting the man

to suppress the call of the Creative Power by becoming lost
in the group. The individual remains free to listen and
respond to the call of the group. As a matter of fact,
the more the call of the Divine hounds the man who has fallen
into inauthenticity, the more tenaciously he may identify
with the group.

Finally, the divine summons breaks through and the man
in a state of inauthenticity listens. He is informed by the
summons that he is living inauthentically, that he is not
realizing his possibilities, that he is lost in the herd.
He comes to realize that he has lost his identity, that he
has not become who he is capable of becoming, that he has not
arrived at his convictions from within himself, but rather
he has had his convictions imposed on him by the group.
Furthermore, he realizes his security in the group was only
illusionary, that if he is to find security in this world,
he must discover it by aligning himself with the Eternal.
He knows that he has lost his freedom, for he has lost the
ability to choose. He has become a slave to the masses.

As he begins to rely on the summons of the divine and to
follow its voice, he begins to reclaim the ability to choose;
thus, he regains his freedom. He learns to express his convictions which come from the Divine Ground, even if they are
critical and contrary to the views of the group. He reclaims
the ability to choose and to speak for himself. He becomes
free to rise above the "average," the "herd"; he is free to

transform the world if he can. The divine summons, then, informs the inauthentic man that he is escaping from himself by conforming to the group. It also points the way for the inauthentic man to live authentically. Each time he listens to the voice of the Divine and acts according to this morally sensitive summons, he reaffirms his true self, which makes it easier for him to reject the call of the group.

2. The Judge-Penitent

Having summarized the abstract concepts about inauthentic and authentic existence, we shall now look to some contemporary stories to develop this more fully.

In dealing with the problem of suffering, we considered Albert Camus' The Plague. Now, as we attempt to deal with the Christian understanding of the two modes of existence and the paradigm of Christ in relationship to the transformation, we shall examine another of Camus' works, The Fall.[1] Although Camus' blik is not the Christian faith, he can assist the Christian in understanding these categories under consideration.

The protagonist in The Fall is a man in his forties who has adopted as his primary vocation that of being a "judge-penitent." His secondary vocation is that of a lawyer, currently with his clients being mostly known crooks. His main

---

[1](New York: Alfred A. Knopf, 1959), tr. by Stuart Gilbert.

place of activity is a bar in Amsterdam which goes under the incongruous name of "Mexico City." Occasionally middle-class visitors patronize this seamy den which is located in a poor section of the city. When the bourgeois tourist comes, Jean Baptiste Clamence engages in conversation with him. Jean Baptiste or John the Baptist is the assumed name of the protagonist, not his real name. A lawyer about the same age as Clamence comes to the bar, and Clamence begins a conversation with him. The conversation is really a monologue, somewhat in the form of a confession. This puts the story into motion.

First of all, Clamence tells the visitor about his past, his previous situation. We shall interpret Clamence's previous existence as being inauthentic. In other words, his existence was extremely shallow. It might even be said that he lived in a "state of innocence," for he was not unlike Adam in the biblical myth, walking around in his Garden of Eden without a knowledge of right and wrong.

In the past, Clamence had been a successful lawyer, for he chose his cases and liked only those which dealt with the widow and orphan. Not indulging in bribery, he enjoyed receiving praise from those he protected. The accused sat before the judges, and he defended them, not having to become deeply involved because he was neither the accused, nor the judge. He simply received the praise from the poor, the widow and the orphan. So he chose those cases which were clean, that would not question his personal integrity, nor make him become passionately involved.

As Clamence was a handsome man and very intelligent, his company was in great demand, and he was invited to most of the important social events. He was an excellent conversationalist, a superb and tireless dancer, and a seasoned lover who enjoyed playing the field. He participated in a variety of sports and tended to excel in them all. In fact, he was such a perfect man that he often felt he was more than man; he was almost a superman.

Clamence enjoyed giving directions to strangers and helping the blind across the street. He admitted, however, that his solicitude was motivated by being seen by other men. Often he would take a blind man by the hand, lead him across a dangerous intersection, and then, as he departed, would tip his hat to the man. Since the man was blind, he obviously could not see the gesture, but those who were standing on the street could. Although he gave his money freely, he had to be the master of his own liberality. He chose noble causes, but only those that could bring him praise.

Furthermore, Clamence acknowledged that he enjoyed high places, looking down on the "human ants" below. Also, from the heights he was easier seen by men. His participation in his profession, his social life, and in life, in general, was such that he received immense pleasure. He thought he had much to offer any situation, although he doubted that others had anything to really contribute to him. He was doing them a favor simply to be present. Since Clamence knew the pleasures that generosity could bring, he was always looking for things to do. Usually he did them before anyone else because he wanted for himself the pleasure they could give. Although he was not religious, he could not help but think that perhaps behind his fortune there was some benevolent power.

From this description, we shall maintain that Clamence was living in a state of inauthenticity. He did not become involved with people, and, although he was extremely selfish, he was subtle enough to allow his selfishness to appear as generosity. On the surface he was thought to be a person who could forgive and forget. If he had a severe disagreement with a person, he might meet him on the street a couple of days later and become nice and friendly as if nothing had happened. The reason he could do this was that he had probably forgotten the man's name and the nature of the altercation. Human beings simply did not mean much to him, except as they could be manipulated to give him pleasure. Of course, while Clamence was living in his bourgeois, secular, Garden of Eden, he did not have a realistic understanding of himself. He did not know how subtle and devious his behavior was. Since he did not remain in this condition, we might well ask: what happened to Clamence to enable him to become aware of

his estranged condition, to become aware of his inauthenticity? What made him realize that he was a phony? It
seems that his conscience began to disturb him as he reacted
to a number of unfortunate situations. One night, as he was
walking alone, feeling pleased with himself, he heard laughter,
but there was no one in sight. Clamence spoke of his experience this way:

> I felt rising within me a vast feeling of power--I don't
> know how to express it--of completion, which cheered my
> heart. I straightened up and was about to light a ciga-
> rette, the cigarette of satisfaction, when, at that very
> moment, a laugh burst out behind me. Taken by surprise,
> I suddenly wheeled around; there was no one there.[1]

Although Clamence was not able to understand the laughter
at that time, it appears to be the beginning of a troubled
conscience. He walked home, and when he went into the bathroom for a glass of water, he said: "My reflection was smiling
in the mirror, but it seemed to me that my smile was double..."

A second experience in Clamence's journey towards self-
awareness took place one evening in a traffic jam. A man on
a motorcycle in front of him could not start his engine, but
rather than move to one side, he remained in the street
blocking traffic. Clamence tried to reason with him to move
over to the side so that the traffic could flow freely, but
the man was very angry and refused. A bystander stepped in,
assuring Clamence that he must not hit the man. Finally the
man started the motorcycle and left, with Clamence standing

---

[1]Ibid., pp. 38-39.

on the street blocking traffic with horns blowing. Clamence

became befuddled. A stranger remarked: "Poor dope." Clamence

realized that he had not been able to maintain his immaculate

image. As he thought about what he should have done, he

realized that what he would have liked to have done was to

strike the man, to get his revenge, and to conquer him. He

then became aware that he broken in public. An anonymous

man had judged him "poor dope." Furthermore, he had felt

some very hostile feelings toward a human being. As Clamence

spoke to the stranger in the bar, he said:

> I learned at last that I was on the side of the guilty,
> the accused, only in exactly so far as their crime caused
> me no hard. Their guilt made me eloquent because I was
> not its victim. When I was threatened, I became not only
> a judge in turn but even more; an irascible master who
> wanted, regardless of all laws, to strike down the of-
> fender and get him on his knees. After that, mon cher
> compatriots, it is very hard to continue seriously be-
> lieving one has a vocation for justice and is the pre-
> destined defender of the widow and orphan.[1]

A third experience that contributed to Clamence's self-

awareness involved a woman with whom he was carrying on an

affair. He discovered that she was very passive and that

apparently they were rather incompatible. He dropped her and

thought nothing of it, until he learned that she had told a

third party about his inadequacies. Immediately he sought to

renew the affair in order to vent his hostility. He re-

established the relationship and became somewhat cruel, but

finally was able to drop the woman again when he discovered

---

[1]Ibid., pp. 55-56.

that she was a masochist and that she was using his hostility to satisfy her abnormal needs.

The final experience, which enabled the conscience to tell Clamence who he was, took place one night about an hour past midnight. Clamence had just left the bed of a mistress "who was already asleep" and walked over a bridge on his way to his apartment. He saw a woman standing on the bridge looking down at the water. He walked past her. After he had gone about fifty yards, he heard her body strike the water in the silence of the night. He was torn between helping her and going home. He heard her screams but decided to go home. He then refused to read a newspaper for several days, for he did not wish to learn for certain what the outcome was. Clamence, however, was unable to forget about this experience; it continued to disturb his conscience.

From these various experiences Clamence arrived at a new understanding of himself. He came to realize that life was not nearly as simple as he had thought, even he was most complex. He was like a Janus; he was two-faced. The face that he showed to the public was that of a generous, good-natured man. The face that really represented him was that of an egotistical and selfish man. His experience in the traffic jam and with the masochist revealed that he had within his own nature the need to dominate and destroy. Both incidents clearly revealed to him that others are always judging. The man on the street said: "Poor dope." The masochist remarked that he was inadequate. Both were judgments passed on Clamence. Finally, his own conscience was hounding and judging him. His authentic conscience was laughing at his inauthentic self. His conscience was telling him he was guilty. Not only did he have the desire to destroy, but he had failed to save, for he had refused to save the woman who had committed suicide. The water was simply too cold and the risk was too great to jump in after her; but for his refusing to act, he paid with an uneasy conscience. It seemed at times as if the whole universe was laughing at him. Over and over again he heard that same body hit the water. He could no longer live his simple life, for he had been touched where it really matters. People and threatening experiences had penetrated his armor, destroying his self-satisfaction.

No longer able to live in the security of his secular version of the Garden of Eden, in a state of inauthenticity, Clamence now attempted to become authentic. At first he sought to destroy the reputation he had established; so in court he attempted to expose the crimes of the honest man in order to protect the dishonest man. His reasoning was that if all the dishonest men were convicted, then the honest men would continue to think they were innocent and not guilty.

Attempting to be in love, Clamence again was disillusioned, for he discovered that women knew how to talk of love but not how to love. He was convinced that genuine love might be experienced three or four times every century. After his failure to love and be loved, he tried to live in a state of chastity but was unsatisfied with living alone. Then he turned to debauchery. In fact, he was living with a mature prostitute and a woman of the best society at the same time. He tired of the prostitute and the other woman married a man of her own social class. With lewd women and alcohol Clamence was deadening his vitality and likewise his capacity to suffer. He was becoming numb and oblivious to life.

But finally he discovered his vocation of the judge-penitent, his discovery coming in a most unusual way. During the Second World War he was placed in a prisoner of war camp in North Africa, where the prisoners were literally dying of hunger and thirst. One prisoner had maintained some semblance of the Christian faith; so the prisoner thought that rather than having a pope who prayed on the throne, they needed a pope who would live among the wretched. As it turned out Clamence was elected pope, with it being his duty to keep alive in memory the sufferings of the men in the event he escaped. As he played the part of pope, he became increasingly serious. He literally became the group leader and the judge. He decided who would receive the extra drink of water, and once he even drank the water of a dying comrade under the guise that the man was going to die anyway; and besides, it was important that he perform his function as pope.

As time passed, Clamence came to the conclusion that

he was the king, pope, and the judge of his own little universe. In other words, if, as he thought, there were no God,
the authority of the king and pope was not based on divine
revelation; thus, they had no real authority. Each man was
his own authority. Clamence, then, was a prophet without
a messiah, an Elijah without a promise of one to come, a
John the Baptist without a Christ. His prophecy was that no
messiah will be sent to this generation. If man is to be
saved, he must become his own messiah; he must save himself,
or else there is no salvation.

The judge-penitent realizes that all men are guilty
because all men judge. Men may not judge by a written law.
It is the law that the individual does not even know that men
judge by. Even Jesus was guilty although he may not have
been guilty of the crimes for which he was accused. It is
reported that, in order to destroy the infant Jesus, Herod
killed children while Jesus and his family escaped to safety.
It was because of Jesus that those children of Israel were
murdered. It was because of Jesus that millions of Abraham's
children have been humiliated and murdered for the past
two thousand years. Surely someone as sensitive as Jesus
would have felt guilty knowing that he had been in some way
responsible for the deaths of others caused by his enemies
as well as by his over-zealous disciples in every generation.
Thus Clamence believes that democracy will come on the scene
when all men realize in some way they are guilty.

Only by judging oneself can the judge-penitent escape
the judgment of others. In judging himself more severely
than others judge him, he can escape the judgment of others.
After he judges himself, he is then free to judge others
and he extends the judgment to others without distinction.
At the same time the penitent reminds us that the judgment
we pass on others usually snaps back in our faces, for eventually we are guilty of the very crimes for which we accuse
others. Since every man some day ends up as a penitent,
Clamence chose to follow the road in the opposite direction,
namely, to be a penitent first and then do his judging or to
do the two simultaneously. The judge-penitent is one who
judges but who also knows at the same time he is guilty and
is judged by others. He not only judges others but also
judges himself. He finds others guilty, but discovers that
he is equally guilty, not necessarily of the same crimes.
The judge-penitent likes confessions. He gives his own confession, expressing how he is the lowest of the low, but he
moves to how "we" are the lowest of the low. If he can entice
the listener to judge himself, he will be free from having
to judge him.

Caums' analysis can assist us in working out more carefully the Christian understanding of existence. In the person
of Clamence, he depicts two ways of existing in the world.
First, Clamence is shallow, blind, egotistical, selfish,
and hedonistic. In his inauthentic state he really does not

understand his situation. Second, after he moves from this original state through the fall, he possesses many of the same characteristics, with the exception that he is no longer blind. He now understands himself in a new way, and he self-consciously chooses his life style. It is only after the fall that he can understand his former existence for what it was, namely an egotistical sham. Now he knows what he is doing and why. Clamence's move from inauthenticity to authenticity, according to Camus, is possible by the exertion of human effort. In other words, man lifts himself up by his own bootstraps although he cannot lift himself too high.

Of course, the Christian can accept the two modes of existence in Camus' analysis, but the total analysis he cannot accept. The major weakness is that the Christian story reveals that man is both worse and potentially better than Camus' analysis will allow. Man, estranged from God, is indeed in a state of inauthenticity. His condition is so serious that he cannot possibly begin to overcome it by human effort alone. Man must have a mediator who can not only reveal to him his desperate situation but point the way for overcoming it. The Christian believes that such a mediator exists, and he is the Christ. It is through the Christ as revealed, as preached about, as present in ritual and sacrament that God's grace is mediated to man. Hence it is the mediator that enables man to move from a state of in-authenticity to authenticity. The state of authenticity is potentially higher than that envisioned by Camus because the power to attain it is derived from the Creative Power in the universe and not in human effort alienated from this Power. So what is lacking in Camus' analysis is the dimension of transcendence and a way of mediating that transcendence to man; or, to be more specific, what is lacking is the paradigm of Christ, and from the perspective of the Christian story, this is a serious omission.

3. The Non-Conformist

In 1963, Ken Kesey published his popular novel One Flew Over The Cuckoo's Nest,[1] and in the same year Dale Wasserman adapted it for the broadway stage. Although the original production was rather poor, the novel is good, and it can aid us in our attempt to find an appropriate paradigm of Christ in modern literature.

Kesey's story takes place inside a large public mental hospital located in the far West. Although the setting is a hospital for people who cannot function adequately on their own in society, we should not interpret his story as being solely about psychotics. The hospital simply provides an adequate vehicle for presenting his message. The patients are plagued by many of the same problems that we all face. Thus, Kesey is attempting to make a statement about man, not just men who are hospitalized in a mental institution. Many

---

[1](New York: Signet Books, 1963).

of his concerns could be placed in a business, political, educational, or even an ecclesiastical setting. So there is a sense in which he is talking about "out there" but there is another sense in which he is talking about "right here." In other words, he has sought to reduce the world and its problems to a mental hospital.

The narrator of the story is an American Indian who is the son of an Indian chief and a white woman. He tells us that his father had been forced to sell the Indian lands to the government so that a hydro-electric power plant could be erected. He also thinks his mother helped to destroy the integrity of his father. The outcome of the father's harmful experiences is that he ends up a drunk, a nothing. Following one year in college, the narrator entered the mental hospital. When he first came to the hospital, everyone thought he was deaf and dumb, so he was allowed to overhear all kinds of confidential conversations. Eventually, he informs us that he regained the strength to come out of his shell and become a person again through his relationship with a patient by the name of McMurphy. Through his relationship with this unusual man, he overcomes his retreat from reality, votes to see the world series on television, goes on a fishing trip, fights a sadistic orderly, and finally escapes from the hospital.

However, we soon discover the protagonist in the story is not the narrator but McMurphy. Prior to his arrival at the hospital, McMurphy had been given a six month prison sentence for gambling and assault. Because he did not like the food, nor the work, and had won all the inmates' money, he fakes a psychosis in order to be sent to the mental hospital. McMurphy is a thirty-five year old, red-headed Irishman, who is full of life and has a passion for gambling.

To make an understatement, the action begins when Mc-Murphy enters the ward of the mental hospital. Immediately the patients sense that he is not the run of the mill psychotic. Rather than coming in frightened and withdrawn, he steps forward with a big genuine smile, shaking everyman's hand. When he looks at the Indian, he immediately perceives that his maladies are a fake. When he meets the Big Nurse, who is in charge of the ward, he sees right through her; he knows that underneath her smile, there is a rigid person, made of knife metal.

It does not take long for McMurphy to learn that the ward follows a very rigid schedule. Noting that most of the men are passive and lifeless, he soon discovers why; for the Big Nurse sits behind a glass cage nurses' station and runs the ward like a dictator. Even the doctor is a mouse-like man who gives in to the wishes of the nurse. There are three sadistic male helpers who assist her in keeping the men frightened. Furthermore, she does not hesitate to use fear to keep the men in line. She lets them know that if they do not play by her rules of the game they might well end up a vegetable as the result of^R premature lobotomy. And, if they get out of line, she usually has her say about who gets electric shock therapy. In addition, she can prescribe the medications; thus, she has ominous power over the patients.

Her ward is spic and span. Everything moves on schedule, and nothing can change it. So the men jump to it when she speaks. There are some women who can bring out the masculinity in a man. The Big Nurse is not this kind of a woman. In fact, she takes away from the men their manhood. In a psychological sense she emasculates her patients, so that the men in her ward become passive, zombie-like and dead as human beings. In other words, they adjust to her deadly situation.

As McMurphy is a man very much alive, we sense at once that there will be trouble. Almost immediately he attempts to take over the ward. Through manipulations, he acquires a lounge which the men use for gambling. He organizes a basketball team, arranges for several of the patients to go on a fishing trip with a young woman of questionable character, and even slips two prostitutes into the ward one night. Although McMurphy is certainly unconventional, he does have a therapeutic influence on the ward. Several men become able to leave the hospital, and others are transferred to less severe wards. The ward becomes a place of life and excitement. Patients, who were dead as human beings, become alive.

But McMurphy was not able to accomplish all of this without a great cost to himself. He started his contest with the Big Nurse as a result of a bet that he made with a man that "he could get her goat." Although he won the bet, battle after battle followed. It was a fierce combat between the free red-headed Irishman and the Big Nurse who was determined to get him on his knees, so that she could control him as she had managed the others. Until the very end, McMurphy remained a free man although he was turned into a vegetable.

When he first arrived on the ward, McMurphy helped the patients in order to con them out of their money and cigarettes, but later he aids them out of a kind of human compassion. In time they begin to respond to his humane treatment and genuine concern for them. His life becomes involved with theirs. Seeking to help them, he wants them to truly become men. He has his successes, but he also has his failures. Finally, he ends up fighting one of the sadistic aids who was humiliating another patient. At the same time the Indian enters the fray, taking on another aid. Although the Big Nurse suspects the aid precipitated the fight, she gives McMurphy the opportunity to admit that he was wrong. By such a move, she is trying to destroy his integrity. If he does not admit his guilt, it will be necessary for him to go into shock therapy. This was a big decision for McMurphy, but he refused to submit to the admission demanded by the Big Nurse. He went through three shock sessions. After each, she gave him the opportunity to admit that he was wrong, but he refused.

The final episode, which led to the destruction of
McMurphy, takes place on the morning following a drinking
party in the ward. Outside women of questionable character
had been clandestinely brought into the hospital. After the
party, the patients decide that McMurphy must escape from
the hospital, but before he could leave the Big Nurse and
her aides appeared in the ward and found a young patient
asleep with one of the women of the street. As the young man's
mother was a personal acquaintance of the nurse, and as it
appears that his own mother had been as emasculating to him
as the Big Nurse, the nurse attempts to shame him in the
presence of the patients, threatening to inform his mother
about the affair. She sends him to a vacant doctor's office
and holds McMurphy and the other men responsible for the
young man's waywardness. Alone in the doctor's office, the
young man commits suicide. Although it is obvious the Big
Nurse was the precipitating factor, she holds McMurphy responsible. Realizing that he was now in a desperate situation,
McMurphy makes a last attempt to assault the Nurse, as
members of the staff place him in a straightjacket and cart
him off for brain surgery.

In a couple of weeks McMurphy is returned to the ward
in a wheelchair and as a vegetable. His first night back in
the ward the Indian places a pillow over his face and suf-
focates him with the approval of another patient because they
know it was what McMurphy would want. The Indian then picks

up a piece of heavy equipment and throws it through the window and escapes. Ironically, this method of escape had been planned by McMurphy earlier; thus he had enabled the Indian to regain both his mental health and his physical freedom. The other patient had planned an alibi for the Indian so that the authorities would think that McMurphy had died of complications from the surgery. Thus, they would not make much of an effort to have the Indian return. The story ends with the escape of the Indian.

From this rough summary, we can raise the question about what are the implications of Kesey's rather unusual story. First of all, it seems to me, that he is making an observation that many other writers have made before him. He is saying that life is becoming so organized that human beings are losing their humanness. Kesey obviously feels that the loss of individuality and the pressures for conformity are destructive and even demonic. They destroy a person.

The Indian refers to the dictatorial system as the "Combine." It is present in the hospital and the Big Nurse is its most devoted advocate, but it is also present outside the hospital. When they are driving to the boat for their day of fishing, the Indian makes the following observation about a typical American suburban neighborhood. He says:

> All up the coast I could see the signs of what the Combine had accomplished since I was last through this country, things like, for example--a train stopping at a

station and laying a string of full grown men in mirrored
suits and machined hats, laying them like a hatch of
identical insects, halflife things coming pht-pht-pht
out of the last car, then hooting its electric whistle
and moving on down the spoiled land to deposit another
hatch...Or things like five thousand houses punched
out identical by a machine and strung across the hills
outside town, so fresh from the factory they're still
linked together like sausages...[1]

Kesey then is maintaining that our society is sick.
This, I believe, is one of the reasons he chose a mental
hospital for his setting. Thus, for a man to get along in
a sick society, he must be or become sick. If a man is not
sick, the Combine will beat him into conformity, forcing
him to shape up. Since it is the society which determines
what is normal and what is abnormal, if a society is sick
and run by sick men, then sickness becomes normalcy and a
lack of sickness becomes abnormalcy. We might recall that
Ionesco came to a similar conclusion in Rhinoceros, and
Erich Fromm in his well known work Escape From Freedom says:
"The person who gives up his individual self and becomes an
automaton, identical with millions of other automatons
around him, need not feel alone and anxious any more. But
the price he pays, however, is high; it is the loss of his
self."[2]

Secondly, and perhaps most important for our study,
McMurphy is a kind of secular messiah. He is a man, an
individualist, a non-conformist; so he has trouble with the

---

[1] Ibid., p. 203.

[2] (New York: Rinehart and Co., 1941), p. 186.

Combine. At one time he had received the Distinguished
Service Cross in Korea for having led an escape from a communist prison camp, but he later received a dishonorable
discharge for insubordination. Furthermore, McMurphy is a
free man and very much alive. In many respects he embodies
what a man can be. Even his freedom and aliveness are contagious, for men who had been dead as human beings--some
for as long as twenty years--become infected with his freedom
and love of life. They become men again.

But the same thing happens to McMurphy that happens to
most messiahs, whether they be religious or secular ones.
As always, messiahs threaten the established order. They
upset too many applecarts, so they have to be cooled. Just
as Socrates drank his hemlock, Jesus went to his cross, and
Martin Luther King, Jr., was gunned down, McMurphy, the
secular messiah, has received his kiss of death. When he is
placed on the table for shock therapy, he is stretched out
somewhat like a man being crucified. Rather than receiving
a crown of thorns, he has placed on his head the instruments
for electric shock. As it turns out, this was not enough,
so finally he receives the full treatment with the lobotomy.
Now he is really fixed. He will not bring life and freedom
to anyone else. He will never give anyone else a moment's
trouble, for he is a vegetable. However, his disciples will
not allow him to be an instrument or show piece for what
happens to free men. He will not be a public example for

forcing men to give up their freedom. Hence they take the life of a vegetable, not McMurphy, so the Combine is deprived of its number one exhibit.

Obviously Kesey's story more closely approaches the Christian story than does the story of Camus. When Kesey refers to the Combine and its ill effects on human beings, he is approximating certain aspects of the Christian understanding of man's existence after the fall. In the midst of fallen humanity, there are still people who have a capacity to retain their individuality and assert their freedom. Hence there is implicit within this story at least two modes of existence, which we designated earlier as inauthentic and authentic. In Kesey's characters, who express a kind of authenticity, there is not the cynicism and abandonness that we find in Camus. Hence in this respect he is closer to the Christian story also.

However, where Kesey most closely approaches the Christian story is in the character of McMurphy. McMurphy comes into the human situation, the mental hospital, and finds suffering and inauthentic humanity. Through his relationship with the patients, he has a therapeutic and reconciling effect. He enables many of them to return to a kind of authenticity, that is, to understand themselves, to assert their freedom, and to become men again. Hence McMurphy is the link which enables the patients to move from one mode of existence to another. Such a view obviously approximates the Christian story.

One aspect of the character of Jesus was that he was a free man, and he came into an unfree world. His freedom threatened some unfree men, so they destroyed him. But his freedom was also contagious, and some unfree men became infected by the germ. As the infection spread throughout their bodies and penetrated their very selves, they too became free men, his disciples. In a similar way, McMurphy was a free man who experienced his own type of martyrdom because of it, but he also passed the infection of freedom on to others. They became free and lived to tell the story as in the case of the Indian.

Nevertheless, it does not seem that Kesey's story is completely acceptable to the Christian. For one thing, McMurphy's promiscuous sexual behavior will not be acceptable to many Christians as depicting an adequate paradigm of Christ. McMurphy not only, at times, exploited his male colleagues he also exploited his female acquaintances. But the most important weakness of McMurphy as a paradigm of Christ is the dimension of transcendence. There is a vague suggestion of a "this world transcendence" in that McMurphy and his authentic disciples transcend the bonds of the dehumanizing Combine. Yet, this transcendence is very limited. There is no indication of "another world transcendence" which is as much a part of the Christian story as is a "this world transcendence." In other words, there is no

real element of mystery or resurrection, except within a narrow
naturalism which Christianity can never fully embrace. Or
to phrase it differently, Kesey's faith is still faith in
man, not in man's Creator.

4. The Unidentified Guest

As we continue our search for an appropriate paradigm
of Christ, we shall now consider T. S. Eliot's The Cocktail
Party.[1] This work is an English comedy of manners having
a conventional structure. It is made up of three acts, broken
down into five scenes. The first act takes place in the
London apartment of Edward and Lavinia Chamberlayne. Edward
is a middle-aged barrister. He and Lavinia have been married
for five years, but they have never had any children. Edward
holds a cocktail party, but Lavinia is conspicuously absent.
At the party there is a mysterious, unidentified guest.
After the guests have left, Edward confides to the unidentified
guest that Lavinia has left him. However, the guest assures
Edward that his wife will return if he wishes it. As the
conversation continues, Celia, an attractive younger woman,
returns to the apartment, and we learn that Edward has been
having an affair with her. Still later, even Lavinia and
other guests return as the result of receiving a mysterious
telegram.

The second act takes place in a psychiatrist's office.

---

[1](New York: Harcourt, Brace and Co., 1950).

We discover that the psychiatrist was the unidentified guest in act one, and that he and both Alex and Julia, who were also present at the original party, are working together in some way. Edward comes to the psychiatrist for help, then Lavinia, and finally Celia. When each leaves his office, each has made an important decision.

The third act again takes place in the Chamberlaynes' London apartment, with preparations being made for another cocktail party. Just before the party begins, the same guests who were present at the original party drop in with the exception of Celia. The play ends with these guests leaving, and with Edward and Lavinia preparing to receive others.

It is our contention that The Cocktail Party is a self-conscious and distinctive Christian drama. We make this assertion for three reasons. First of all, Eliot was a Christian. He was an Anglo-Catholic-Christian and he let it be known. Often he wrote about Christian subjects, e.g. Murder In The Cathedral and The Idea of a Christian Society. Secondly, Christian language is dispersed throughout The Cocktail Party. Terms such as atone, salvation, crucifixion, and sin are used. Reference is made to the parable of the Good Samaritan. Words such as light and darkness, sight and blindness remind us somewhat of the language of the Gospel of John. Thirdly, and most important, the message of the drama is Christian. In fact, it appears that Eliot has attempted to translate the Christian gospel into a secular and contemporary idiom. If he has not demythologized the gospel, he has at least remythologized it in such a way that it has become more contemporary.

As we maintained in the section on "The Normative Story," the Christian story is a story with three parts. Likewise, Eliot is saying that the Christian drama of salvation is a play with three acts. It begins with the human condition. People are estranged from themselves, from one another, and from God. The human condition is reflected in the persons of Edward, Lavinia, Celia, and Peter. For example, in act one, Edward and the unidentified guest are talking, and the guest says:

> . . . There's a loss of personality;
> Or rather, you've lost touch with the person
> You thought you were. You no longer feel quite human.
> You're suddenly reduced to the status of an object--
> A living object, but no longer a person.[1]

A few moments later, Edward asks: "To what does this lead?" And the guest replies:

> To finding out
> What you really are. What you really feel.
> What you really are among other people.
> Most of the time we take ourselves for granted,
> As we have to, and live on a little knowledge
> About ourselves as we were. Who are you now?
> You don't know any more than I do,
> But rather less. You are nothing but a set
> Of obsolete responses. The one thing to do
> Is to do nothing. Wait......
>
> Resign yourself to the fool you are.
> That's the best advice I can give you.[2]

---

[1] Ibid., p. 29.

[2] Ibid., p. 31.

So Edward at first does not understand himself, but he comes

to realize that something is wrong with him. In a conver-

sation with Celia, he says:

> It would need someone greater than the greatest doctor
> To cure this illness.[1]

Celia then asks Edward what it is that he wants, and he

replies:

> I am not sure.
> The one thing of which I am relatively certain
> Is, that only since this morning
> I have met myself as a middle-aged man
> Beginning to know what it is to feel old.[2]

Celia also notes that her perception of Edward has begun to

change. She explains:

> I listened to your voice, that had always thrilled me,
> And it became another voice--no, not a voice:
> What I heard was only the noise of an insect,
> Dry, endless, meaningless, inhuman--
> You might have made it by scraping your legs together--
> Or however grasshoppers do it. I looked,
> And listened for your heart, your blood;
> And saw only a beetle the size of a man
> With nothing more inside it than what comes out
> When you tread on a beetle.[3]

These passages illustrate what Eliot believes the human

condition to be. To be a sinner is to be a man without God,

and without God man does not know who he is. He is able to

be married to a woman for five years, as in the case of

Edward and Lavinia, without knowing her. He is disoriented

---

[1] Ibid., p. 61.

[2] Ibid., p. 65.

[3] Ibid., pp. 66-67.

and does not know which way to turn. Losing the power to be a man, he becomes like Kafka's gigantic insect. He loses his humanness.

Act one then presents the human condition. It reveals a situation in which God is not directly present. It is somewhat like the Christian understanding of the Old Testament situation: man is in need of a messiah, but there is no messiah.

Before moving directly to act two, an interpretation of the psychiatrist might be offered. In act one there is an unidentified guest who becomes identified in the second act. He is Henry Harcourt-Reilly, a psychiatrist. Throughout the play, he is aloof and somewhat mysterious. In fact, those who encounter him are not sure whether he is some kind of a devil or whether he is truly good. They are not exactly sure what they are to make of him. It is our contention that Harcourt-Reilly is the paradigm of Christ. In act one, he is unidentified, but he is present at the cocktail party. Eliot might well be implying that God is not only present in religious activities on the Sabbath, but that he is present in secular activities throughout the week, even at cocktail parties. Although Harcourt-Reilly was originally incognito, he was still present, concerned, and accomplishing his purpose. It might be noted that this Christ paradigm drinks gin and water rather than grape juice.

If act one depicts the human condition, then act two

offers the means for coping with it. In other words, it
becomes a time of grace and salvation. Now Edward goes to
the secular church at the appointed hour, the church being the
psychiatrist's office and the hour being eleven o'clock.
When Edward enters the consulting room, he immediately discovers that Sir Henry Harcourt-Reilly is the psychiatrist
who was the unidentified guest at the party. In the consul-
tation, Edward confesses that he no longer can believe in
his own personality and that he has become obsessed with the
thought of his own insignificance. Then Edward explains:

> I am not afraid of the death of the body,
> But this death is terrifying. The death of the spirit--
> Can you understand what I suffer?
>
> . . . I can no longer act for myself.
> Coming to see you--that's the last decision
> I was capable of making. I am in your hands.
> I cannot take any further responsibility.[1]

When Edward has completed his confession, Sir Henry
invites Lavinia, who has been waiting in the sitting room,
to come in. Hence the husband and wife are forced to confront
each other. Both come to realize that they have been decep-
tive and dishonest in their relations with each other.
During the honest encounter, it is disclosed that Edward has
been having his affair with Celia and that Lavinia had known
it all along, although she had not let Edward know that she
knew. It is also revealed that Lavinia has been carrying on
an affair with Peter, but Edward had not known about it.

---

[1]Ibid., p. 113.

Since Peter's attention had turned from Lavinia to Celia,
a crisis had developed for Lavinia. This accounts for her
absence at the cocktail party. Thus, it turns out that
Edward thought that he was incapable of loving, for he had
never really loved Lavinia and there was question about whether
he had actually loved Celia. On the other hand, Lavinia
thought that she was incapable of being loved, that no one
could love her. The fact that Edward had been unfaithful to
her and that Peter was dropping her for Celia tended to con-
firm her fear. So Edward's inability to love and Lavinia's
inability to be loved were threats to their self-esteem.
Through the aid of Sir Henry, they realize they are meant
for each other in that their weaknesses complement each other.
They decide to make the best of a bad situation. As the couple
depart from the office, having resolved to give their marriage
another try, Sir Henry pronounces his secular benediction:

> My secretary will send you my account.
> Go in peace. And work out your salvation with diligence.[1]

The second act is not only a period of grace, a time of
reconciliation for Edward and Lavinia; it is also a time of
grace for Celia. Shortly after the Chamberlaynes' departure,
Celia comes to Sir Henry. She too recognizes him as the
mysterious unidentified guest at Edward's party. She explains
to the psychiatrist that something is either wrong with herself
or there is something wrong with the world. As she cannot

---

[1]Ibid., p. 128.

believe that something is wrong with the world, she believes
that her problem resides with her. Lately she has become
aware of a kind of solitude and aloneness. Although she
thought that she had been able to relate to and communicate
with people, she realizes that she really has not been able
to at a meaningful level. Not only does she feel that she is
alone, but she believes that all people are if they would
only admit it. She explains:

> No...it isn't that I want to be alone,
> But that everyone's alone--or so it seems to me.
> They make noises, and think they are talking to each
> other;
> They make faces, and think they understand each other.
> And I'm sure they don't...[1]

Celia continues her confession by acknowledging that she
feels a sense of sin. By sin she does not necessarily feel
that she has done an immoral act. She does not even think
that her relationship with Edward was immoral as such. In
fact, her sense of sin is not the result of anything she has
done. Rather it is more a kink, or an emptiness, or a failure
toward someone or something outside herself. Because of this
sense of sin, she feels that she must atone for it.

Sir Henry points out to Celia, as he did to Edward and
Lavinia earlier, that there are two ways open to her. However, she will have to choose which way is best for her. The
path she follows will be her own choice. First, there is the
way the Chamberlaynes chose, that is, to settle down with

---

[1]Ibid., p. 134.

each other and have a family. This is the route most people
follow. Edward and Lavinia now know they do not understand
each other, and they will breed children they do not understand and who will not understand them. Those who follow
this path at least know that they do not understand each
other, and they no longer can live with the delusion that they
do understand. Second, there is the way of the saint. This
road takes courage. Since the way is unknown, it requires
faith, not naive faith, but the kind of faith that rises from
the depths of despair. Which way is best? It would appear
that Eliot affirms the Protestant doctrine of vocation, for
Luther once said that the housewife going about her domestic
chores was doing as much the will of God as the pious monk
in his cubicle. Eliot puts it this way. Neither way is better.
Both are necessary. Each must make his choice.

Unlike Edward and Lavinia, Celia decides to follow the
path of the saint. She admits she does not know what she is
doing, nor why she is doing it. She knows only that she is
doing it. As Celia leaves, having made an important decision,
Sir Henry again pronounces his benediction:

> Go in peace, my daughter.
> Work out your salvation with diligence.[1]

With the salvation of both the Chamberlaynes and Celia
completed, Sir Henry has accomplished what he was sent to do,
so he asserts the familiar words of Jesus on Good Friday:

---

[1]Ibid., p. 145.

"It is finished."

This brings us now to the final act of the drama. It is the time period following the period of grace. It is the period in which the individual must live out his life between reconciliation and the end. The action returns to the Chamberlaynes' London apartment, two years later. The Chamberlaynes are busily preparing for another cocktail party. In some of the productions, though not all, Lavinia is pregnant, indicating that something has resulted from their reconciliation. As the couple talk, we sense there is a new appreciation of one another; they are kinder and are getting along even better than might be expected. In a sense they are now mirrors to one another, for they no longer can live with their old deceptions. Each understands better the motivations of the other. So they are doing a good job in making the best of a bad situation.

Several guests arrive before the scheduled time of the party. In fact, all the guests are present that were present at the original party, with the exception of Celia. Even Peter, who had gone to America and had become very successful in the movie industry, is there. Of course, Peter is the former lover of Lavinia, and had left her for Celia. He is the one who raises the question about Celia's absence. Alex, who had been working on the island of Kinkanja, tells them that Celia is dead. According to his account, she had joined a nursing order and was helping some natives on Kinkanja who were dying of pestilence. An insurrection broke out, and Celia refused to escape wishing to remain with her sick patients. She was captured and was crucified near an ant hill. As Alex concludes the gruesome story, Lavinia comments that Sir Henry did not seem shocked by Celia's death, nor even the way she died. Sir Henry opines that he knew she was under the sentence of death; he simply did not know the method. As both Edward and Lavinia express the feeling that they have some responsibility for Celia's death, Sir Henry tries to dispel their guilt.

As these familiar guests depart, the Chamberlaynes ready themselves and their apartment for the arrival of others. Although Lavinia feels that she cannot go through with it, Edward assures her that each moment is a new beginning. Life is simply keeping on. When the curtain falls, the audience receives the impression that Edward and Lavinia will keep on.

5. Conclusion

From our analysis of these three stories, our understanding of the Christian story has been greatly enhanced. In man's alienation from the Creator, he experiences sin, suffering, and death. As he confronts these aspects of the human condition two different modes of existence open before him as possibilities. He can live either inauthentically or authentically. Through the Creator's revelation and reconciliation in the

Christ, man receives the grace and power to move from one
mode of existence to another. In The Fall, Camus depicts
clearly the two modes of existence, but he fails to acknowledge the need for the dimension of divine transcendence
and the necessity of a mediator. Kesey, in One Flew Over
The Cuckoo's Nest, implies, but does not carefully analyze,
the two modes of existence. He focuses on the need for a
mediator, but he does not accept the need for divine transcendence. Eliot best understands and advocates the salient
features of the Christian story. His analysis of inauthentic existence as experienced by the Chamberlaynes and Celia,
and the need for a mediator as exemplified in the character
of the unidentified guest are indeed on target. In his presentation of the character of Sir Henry, he is able to convey
the mystery, omnipresence, and transcendence of the mediator.
He even suggests the significance of discipleship in the
characters of Alex and Julia, who are "guardians" leading
the inauthentic to the source of authenticity. Within the
mode of authenticity, he suggests the possibility of different
life styles. One can opt for the ordinary as did Edward and
Lavinia, or one can seek to become a saint as did Celia.
Although Eliot does not unite suffering with the reconciliation
brought by the mediator, he does suggest that it is an important part of Christian existence. It is implicit in the
Chamberlaynes choosing to make the best of a bad situation,
and it is most obvious in Celia's crucifixion. Of the three

authors examined, it is evident that Eliot's The Cocktail
Party, a comedy, best approximates the Christian understanding
of existence. The unidentified guest, though not perfect,
is an adequate paradigm of Christ.

CHAPTER VIII

THE SILENCE OF GOD

In this study we have established a point of view in which the Christian story is the normative story. From this perspective, we have examined the human condition and correlated it with the answer provided in the Christian story. Now, there is one final problem which at least must be acknowledged; it is the problem of religious skepticism, expressed in its most recent sophisticated form in the death of God theology. There are many today who maintain that God is dead. Some who make this proclamation do it from an immature and anthropocentric view of God. This view of God is incongruous with the modern world. However, this type of God is really an idol and the death of idols is a good thing, for it can prepare the way for genuine faith. However, there are others who have experienced the absence of the true God, and they, too, infer from their experience that He is dead. In my attempt to deal with this problem, I wish to suggest that we look at it from the perspective of the event of Good Friday and Easter. By entertaining the problem from this vantage point, I believe another inference might be drawn from the experience of the absence of God; namely, God is not experienced by some people today, not because he is dead, but because he is silent. Hence it is the silence of God that we need to understand and not his death.

1. Good Friday

For the Christian, the most tragic moment in history is the death of Jesus of Nazareth. The Gospel of Matthew presents in a naked and bold way the depth of the tragedy. As Jesus was dying on the cross, he cried out: "My God, my God, why hast thou forsaken me?"[1] And then Matthew reports: "And Jesus cried again with a loud voice and yielded up his spirit."[2] Matthew's account of the death of Jesus is shocking, for he tells us that in Jesus' greatest hour of need he felt forsaken by God. He also informs us that while Jesus was in the depths of despair he died.

This picture of Jesus' death presented by Matthew is the most moving of the four gospels. He depicts for us the physical suffering of Jesus. Before the procession to the crucifixion site had begun, Jesus had already been severely beaten. He had been mocked by having a crown of thorns, which tore his flesh, forced on his forehead. As he dragged the heavy cross through the streets of Jerusalem, he became physically exhausted. When he reached the place for his execution, his flesh was driven to the cross. He hung on the cross from about twelve o'clock at noon until three

---

[1]Matthew 27:46.

[2]Matthew 27:50

o'clock that afternoon when he died. To state it bluntly, Jesus suffered physically.

But Jesus also suffered mentally. It could be that the mental suffering he endured was vastly greater than his physical suffering. Peter, his most trusted disciple, had denied him three times, and his other disciples had fled during his hour of need. They were cowards, and he knew it. They also had misunderstood him, and this must have greatly disturbed him. At times, there were doubts in Jesus' own mind about his message. There were times in his ministry when he thought the Kingdom of God would come during his life-time, but, now, he knew that he would never live to see it realized. However, the greatest mental agony of Jesus was the result of the silence of God. So Jesus was in despair, and he felt rejected. He not only thought he had been re-jected by man, but he also thought he had been rejected by God. In his moment of greatest need, he cried out to his Heavenly Father, but God remained silent.

2. Silence and Theism

The phrase "the silence of God" contains intrinsically within it a theistic understanding of the nature of God. The theist conceives of God as having the following character-istics. First, God is viewed as <u>personal</u>. He is not the sum total of the stuff the universe is composed of, nor is he a speculative hypothesis to explain how the world first began.

He is personal in the sense that he cares about persons and
can enter into relationships with them through divine-human
encounters. A second characteristic about God is that he is
all-powerful. He has the power to do anything that is
consistent with his nature, for he is able to do anything he
wishes. This implies a third characteristic; namely, he has
freedom. God is free to act or he is free not to act. His
action is determined by his own volition; it is not at the
mercy of every beckoning call of man. A fourth characteristic is that he loves man. We may not know what God's love
is, but we do know what human love is. Hence God's love must
be infinitely greater than man's. In other words, God is no
spider-god, who seeks to torture man. He loves man, which
means he cares about him. Finally, history is the arena
in which God works out his purposes for man. History then is
not simply one "damn thing after another." Behind the apparent
chaos and large amounts of suffering, God is moving man toward some goal. So God is not far removed from history,
but rather he is present in the divine-human drama, even though
he be there incognito. His silence is not indifference,
but it is purposeful.

Yet knowing that God is personal, all-powerful, free,
and loving adds to the tragedy of Jesus' death. For God, the
Father, with all of his power, with all his freedom, and with
all his love, chose to remain silent during the death of his
son. There must have been divine agony within the being of

God himself, as he chose to remain silent while his son was
going through the physical and mental suffering of the crucifixion. It is no wonder that darkness covered the earth
from the sixth to the ninth hour, for God remained silent
in the presence of the death of his son.

However, the divine silence is not limited to Jesus'
tragic death. There have been nations which have experienced
the silence of God, and there have been historical periods
in which God has held his tongue. Hochhuth vividly points
to this experience of the Jew in The Deputy. So men in almost every age have sensed the divine silence. It has plagued
the non-religious man, but it has been experienced by the
saint as well.

As we have noted, today, there are many in Western
civilization who sense God's silence. Ionesco has reminded
us that because we are so busy and loquacious, we are never
quiet long enough to realize whether God is speaking or whether
he is silent. We are so actively speaking ourselves that
we could not even hear God if he were attempting to speak to
us. Likewise, if God is silent, our own voices are so loud
and continuous that God's silence is filled with human
gibberish. Thus, we often confuse our chit-chat with the
voice of God. Whereas, it might well be that God is presently
silent.

3. Waiting for God to Speak

Many of the art forms in our culture reveal the silence of God. The silence is proclaimed in the stories told by the literary artists. This is seen in both drama and the movie. Samuel Beckett, in his tragic-comedy, Waiting For Godot,[1] has obviously experienced the silence. Two of the characters, Estragon and Vladimir, are tramps who are symbols for modern humanity. They do not know what day it is; nor what time it is. They are not sure what they did yesterday, nor what they will be doing tomorrow. They only know they are standing near a dead tree waiting for something or somebody whose name they think might be Godot.

While they are waiting for this mysterious Godot, Pozzo and Lucky come on the scene. These two characters add to Beckett's pathetic understanding of man. Pozzo is wealthy and well-fed. He has a rope tied around Lucky's neck. He jerks the rope and shouts all kinds of abusive language at his servant. Lucky carries two suitcases which he has held so long that his back is bent, and he cannot even place the luggage on the ground while he is resting. In fact, he goes to sleep while holding them. Shortly, Pozzo awakens Lucky with a strong pull on the rope and with a loud shout. Being a faithful and obedient servant, Lucky sets up a table for his master who enjoys his food while Lucky sleeps and the two

---

[1](New York: Grove Press, 1954).

tramps look on. After the sumptious meal, Lucky and Pozzo pick up stakes and depart for the fair where Pozzo expects to sell his servant.

Once the well-stuffed Pozzo is forced to speak, he comes out with a great deal of idiotic, unintelligible phrases. Although at one time he had been very intelligent, he has lost the ability to reason. Pozzo, representing the bodily appetites, has taken over the rational element, represented by Lucky, and the result is the chaotic sounds from the oral cavity of Pozzo. Beckett seems to be saying that we have been too concerned with creature comforts and have neglected the things of the mind and spirit. This neglect has continued so long that the physical appetite has gulped up man's spirit and mind, with only the physical shell remaining.

In any case, the first act comes to an end when a little boy arrives and informs Estragon and Vladimir that Godot will not be able to meet them today, but that he will meet them tomorrow.

The second act is almost a repeat of the first. The two tramps come to the dead tree to wait for Godot. Pozzo and Lucky come again. Only this time, the wealthy Pozzo is blind and Lucky is deaf. Both are pathetic sights. Again the little boy comes to inform the tramps that Godot will not meet them today, but that he will come tomorrow. The futility of waiting finally gets to Estragon and Vladimir, for now they do not believe life is worth living in the face of this futile

ınd endless waiting. They, therefore, attempt to hang themselves with a belt from a limb on the barren tree, but they
ıre a failure because the belt breaks. They are so ineffec-
tive they cannot even escape the eternal waiting by hanging
themselves.

Perhaps the following brief dialogue near the end will
provide some feeling for the mood of the play.

Estragon: (raises the question) Why don't we hang
          ourselves?
Vladimir: With what?
Estragon: You haven't got a bit of rope?
Vladimir: No.
Estragon: Then we can't.

         Silence

Vladimir: Let's go.
Estragon: Wait, there's my belt.
Vladimir: It's too short.
Estragon: You could hang on to my legs.
Vladimir: And who'd hang on to mine?
Estragon: True.
Vladimir: Show all the same. (Estragon loosens the cord
          that holds up his trousers which, much too
          big for him, fall about his ankles. They look
          at the cord.) It might do at a pinch. But
          is it strong enough?
Estragon: We'll soon see. Here.
          (They each take an end of the cord and pull.
          It breaks. They almost fall.)
Vladimir: Not worth a curse.

         Silence

Estragon: You say we have to come back tomorrow?
Vladimir: Yes.

         Silence

Estragon: Didi.
Vladimir: Yes.
Estragon: I can't go on like this.
Vladimir: That's what you think.
Estragon: If we parted? That might be better for us.

```
Vladimir:  We'll hang ourselves tomorrow.  (Pause).
           Unless Godot comes?
Estragon:  And if he comes?
Vladimir:  We'll be saved.[1]
```

If you ask what is the plot of the play, it has no plot, for Beckett thinks that life does not have plot or purpose. If you inquire about the meaning of the play, it says that life is pathetic and pointless. The two tramps think that Godot is important, for their meeting with him might bring meaning and purpose into their lives. But Godot never shows up, and we get the feeling he never will. The two tramps, representing modern man, will go through life waiting for something significant to happen, but it never does.

Beckett is suggesting there are many people today who spend their entire lives waiting--waiting for Godot--or waiting for God, if you like--waiting for something that will bring meaning to their lives. But like the experience of the tramps, Godot does not show up; God does not speak, so their lives remain empty. Many of us do not have to endure the physical suffering of Jesus, but many experience a kind of mental agony. For this reason, we turn to psychiatrists or to drugs or to frenzied, meaningless activity. These are some of the ways we attempt to escape from the silence of God.

So Beckett is speaking about a general problem of Western man, namely, the sense of the loss of meaning in life brought on by an awareness of the silence of God. He depicts the

---

[1]Ibid., pp. 60-61.

condition of Western man in the persons of two hoboes, a
gluttonous, sadistic master, and a submissive slave. The
implication is that many of us feel the silence or absence of
God from our lives, and because of this, life becomes meaningless, and this meaninglessness brings suffering.

4. Living In The Presence Of The Silence

Ingmar Bergman, the movie director and the son of a
Swedish Lutheran pastor, shares Beckett's view, although he
expresses his tragic vision in a different style. This is
apparent in his movie Winter Light. But rather than speaking
generally, Bergman becomes much more personal, for the protagonist in his story is a middle-aged, widowed Lutheran
pastor, Tomas Ericsson.

The movie begins with Tomas giving communion to a handful of people in a small country church. The atmosphere
of the church is as cold as the Swedish winter, and the poor
attendance is indicative of the lack of faith of the pastor.
After the service, a farmer who is severely disturbed about
the prospects of an atomic war, comes to Tomas for guidance.
The farmer has come because his wife believes that Tomas can
help him to deal with his neurotic fear. Rather than helping
the distressed farmer see meaning in life and death, Tomas
becomes a doubting Tomas. He succumbs to an urge to confess
his own doubts about the existence and goodness of God.
Ignoring the desperate needs of the farmer, Tomas says that

God must be either an evil, spider-god or he must not exist
at all. Getting his doubts off his chest helps Tomas, but
it does not help the farmer, for he goes out and shoots himself. After confessing his doubt, Tomas kneels on the floor
of the sanctuary, experiencing a kind of new-found freedom,
as the cold winter light shines through the glass window.
After this experience, Tomas is now able to express himself
freely to Marta Lundberg who is a local school teacher, an
unbeliever, and his mistress. Since the death of his wife,
Marta has been devoted to Tomas. In fact, she wants to marry
him, but he refuses. It appears that Tomas actually detests
her although he cannot get along without her love.

As the day comes to a close, Tomas and Marta drive over
to another little rural church, where the pastor must conduct
a vesper service. Prior to the service, Tomas discusses the
crucifixion with the sexton who is a severe cripple. Obviously having himself in mind, the sexton points out that
many people suffer physically as much as Jesus. He explains
that Jesus' greatest suffering was spiritual, being the result
of God's silence at the crucifixion. Tomas agrees that the
silence of God brings the greatest kind of suffering. When
the time for the services arrives, Tomas goes to the chancel
and stands. The church is empty except for the organist,
the sexton and Marta. Nevertheless, Tomas begins the service
with these words: "Holy, holy, holy, Lord God Almighty.
All the earth is full of his glory ..."[1] With this call to

---

[1] Ingmar Bergman, Three Films (New York: Grove Press,
1970), p. 104, tr. by Paul Britten Austin.

worship, the movie ends.

In various ways, we learn in the movie that Tomas had been happier when his wife was alive and that more people attended church then. It seems, however, that the pastor was receiving strength from his wife's love and faith, not from his own. When she died and he had to rely upon his own spiritual resources, his faith had vanished. Tomas seeks desperately for God to break his silence, but God does not speak.

Tomas, as a minister, is a vivid symbol for the silence of God. The silence is revealed in the small handful of people attending the church; it is seen in the pastor's inability to help the desperate farmer; and it is exemplified again in his inability to return the love of Marta. As a man, Tomas is a prototype for many twentieth century men, for he has grave doubts and a real sense of God's silence. Yet, Tomas still is not able to separate himself completely from God, for he concludes: "Holy, holy, holy, Lord God Almighty..."

Of course, Ingmar Bergman's vision in <u>Winter</u> <u>Light</u> is indeed bleak. For in the presence of the silence of God, man has two alternatives. He can commit suicide as the farmer did, or he can go on living for no apparent reason as Tomas did.

5. <u>Easter</u>

Now let us return to the Christian story about Jesus. We have noted the agony of Jesus as he experienced the silence of God, and we have also noted that this theme is present in many of the literary art forms in our culture. Obviously these forms reveal what many sensitive people experience on a general, abstract level, whereas others experience it on a very personal level. It is the silence of God that intensifies the tragedy of Good Friday; because what Jesus experienced, many of us are beginning to experience.

But let us remember that Good Friday is not the conclusion of the Christian story. For on Easter God broke his silence and spoke. God, the Father, raised his son Jesus from the depths of death. The silence was simply a prelude to the speaking of God. Hence when God spoke, the silence was broken. Death was conquered by life. Hope conquered despair. Cowards became heroes. Men and women who were dead as human beings became alive. So individual lives and history were radically changed. God had broken his silence by speaking clearly and decisively in the resurrection of his son.

Now, what are the implications of Good Friday and Easter for those of us living in a different time and place? These stories remind us that sometimes God is silent, and at other times he chooses to speak. When the Hebrews were in Egyptian slavery, they experienced the divine silence for a while. But in time God broke his silence; for he called Moses, who led the Hebrews out of slavery. God gave them the Torah and established them as a nation. Likewise, in the death of Jesus, God remained silent, but he broke his silence with the Easter faith of the resurrection. Today, we feel that we have reached the end of the road; there is no exit. We sense God's silence. Yet, our hope and our belief, based on Good Friday and Easter, are that eventually God will break his silence again. He will speak to us in a way as meaningful as he did through the Exodus out of Egypt, or as he did in the resurrection of Jesus. Our challenge is to remain attentive and endure the silence without creating false idols or giving up hope.

There have always been periods in history that have been characterized by the voice of God speaking, but there have also been other periods where God has remained silent. With individuals, the experience of both the speaking and silence have been present. Obviously the longer the silence and the greater the awareness of it, the sooner it will be when God will break his silence and speak. It might well be that we are on the verge of having God speak to our age in a way similar to the way he spoke to the first century man with the resurrection of Jesus. It might well be that his speaking will be so powerful that the history of all men who come after us will be influenced by it. As a civilization and as individuals, we must wait patiently, for eventually the divine silence will be broken.

INDEX